Paola Malipiero Art Series

Bruegel

Author: Piero Bianconi

Translator: Murtha Baca

Barron's

Contents

ACKNOWLEDGMENTS

The editors wish to thank for their kind assistance the administrators and directors of the following galleries, institutes, museums, and collections:
Albertina, Vienna
Alte Pinakothek, Munich
Bibliothèque royale Albert Ier, Brussels
Bowdoin College Museum of Art, Brunswick
Boymans-van Beuningen Museum, Rotterdam
Devonshire Collection, Chatsworth Settlement
Doria Pamphili Gallery, Rome
Gallerie Nazioneli di Capodimonte, Naples
Hamburger Kunsthalle, Hamburg
Hessisches Landesmuseum, Darmstadt
Kunsthistorisches Museum, Vienna
Kupferstichkabinett, Berlin
Institute of Arts, Detroit
Louvre, Paris
Mayer van den Bergh Museum, Antwerp
Metropolitan Museum of Art, New York
Musées royaux des Beaux-Arts, Brussels
Narodni Galerie, Prague
National Gallery, London
National Trust, London
Oskar Reinhart Collection, Winterthur
Prado, Madrid
Rijksmuseum, Amsterdam
Soprintendenza Beni Artistici e Storici de lla Campania, Naples
Staatliche Museen, Berlin
Timken Art Gallery, San Diego

Where not otherwise indicated, photographs were provided by the museums or owners.

ILLUSTRATIONS

COLOR PLATES

The Painter and the Connoisseur
Vienna, Albertina

Antwerp in the Sixteenth Century

Pieter Bruegel, called "the Elder" (to distinguish him from his son of the same name), or "Bruegel of the Peasants" (because of his sympathy for the rustic life), was a very highly regarded painter in his day, praised by his many humanist and literary friends, and renowned as the most perfect painter of his generation; he had illustrious protectors and patrons—in short, he was the antithesis of the unknown Romantic genius. And yet we know very little about his life; the number of documents regarding this mysterious character can be counted on the fingers of one hand.

The place and date of Bruegel's birth are not known. We do know that he was admitted to the painters' guild in Antwerp in 1551, but nothing is known about his activities before this date, not even how he came to take up painting.

We also know that Bruegel was in Italy during the years 1551–1553, but very few specifics of his stay there are known.

We know that Bruegel married in 1563 and that he moved from Antwerp to Brussels, but the reasons for this move are unknown; nor do we know the cause of his early death, around the age of forty-five, in September 1569.

We also lack information on what Bruegel's daily life might have been like; thus we must depend almost exclusively on his surviving graphic works and paintings (most of which fortunately can be definitely dated), and, with some reservations, on the biography of Bruegel in Carel Van Mander's *Het Schilderboek* (*Book of Painting*, Haarlem, 1604), which is rather vague and anecdotal.

Thus we know very little about this artist, who is considered not only one of the greatest Flemish painters of the sixteenth century, but also one of the greatest of all time.

Bruegel's birthplace is shrouded in a cloud of mystery. The Florentine Ludovico Guicciardini, in his *Description of All the Low Countries*, published in Antwerp in 1567, two years before Bruegel's death, says that Bruegel was a native of Breda in the Brabant. Van Mander instead wrote that the painter was born in a village near Breda called Bruegel, from which he derived his name, but there is no such village near Breda, which leads us to suspect that Van

Mander invented this rustic birthplace for Bruegel in order to justify the nickname of Bruegel of the Peasants. In fact, the Flemish Vasari wrote: "Nature miraculously discovered a man who would repay her splendidly, when in an obscure village of the Brabant she chose from among the peasants the bright and spirited Pieter Bruegel to be the painter of peasants, for the lasting glory of the Low Countries." In addition, it is quite probable that Van Mander had mistaken a place in Limburg—Brée (which at that time was also spelled Breda)—for Breda in the Brabant.

The question remains unresolved, and two or three villages are still contending for the honor of being the birthplace of Bruegel (like a Flemish Homer); one, in fact, Brögel on the Dommel, has gone so far as to erect a monument to him. At any rate, the generally held opinion today is that Bruegel was not born in the countryside.

The first definite mention of Bruegel dates from 1551, when his name appeared in the *liggeren* (registers) of the Guild of St. Luke in Antwerp, among the *vrymeesters:* "Peeter Brueghels schilder" — that is, "Pieter Bruegel, painter, is declared a master." In that same list appears the name of an Italian, "Joorge Mantewaen, coporen plaetsnyders" ("the Mantuan Giorgio [Ghisi], engraver in copper"), an indication of Antwerp's importance as a center for prints which were circulated throughout the world. From the date of his entrance into the painters' guild we can deduce that Bruegel was born shortly before 1530. The humanist and geographer Abraham Ortelius, an intimate friend of Bruegel's, stated in the latter's epitaph that he had been taken by death *medio aetatis flore,* in the flower of his years, at about forty-five years of age.

Van Mander wrote (and this information is probably accurate) that Bruegel's first teacher was Pieter Coecke Van Aelst (1502–1550), a painter of decorations, a scholar and an architect, a translator of Serlio and Vitruvius — a fashionable artist who had been in Italy and Turkey, and who had succeeded Bernard Van Orley as official painter at the court in Brussels. Vasari wrote: "Pieter Coecke was inventive, and made beautiful cartoons for tapestries, and knew and practiced well the art of architecture; he translated the Bolognese Sebastiano Serlio's work on architecture into the Teutonic language." It is hard to find any influence of Coecke's academic painting in Bruegel's works, but certainly his contact with the rich cultural environment in which Coecke worked and, more importantly, his association with Coecke's wife, the miniaturist Mayken Verhulst Bessemers of Mechlin, were fundamental in the young Bruegel's development. And it is precisely in Mechlin that we have information of Bruegel's early activity.

The young Bruegel's trip to Italy by way of France is documented by, among others, Van Mander: "He went to France and from there to Italy." There are also records of a painting by Bruegel of *Leo of France*. Bruegel began his trip, which lasted two or three years, in 1551, but we do not know his precise itinerary, at least not on the way to Italy. Scholars have surmised that he went through the Rhone Valley (there is a probable recollection of Geneva in *The Harvest*) and that he took a ship from Marseilles to Italy. This hypothesis has never been either borne out or disproven by documentary evidence, but it seems more than plausible and is supported by Bruegel's passion for and knowledge of maritime operations: ships and boats often appear in his paintings, and in a beautiful series of prints entitled *Sea Vessels*. It is certain that Bruegel visited Calabria, Reggio, and the Strait of Messina, as is demonstrated by drawings and prints; slim evidence suggests the possibility that Bruegel also went to Palermo. What is significant about Bruegel's trip is that it was entirely unlike the usual trips made by northern artists to study Italian art of the Renaissance. Bruegel was completely indifferent to Michelangelo and Raphael, and to both ancient and modern Italian monuments; he was never part of the group of Flemish painters who imitated Roman or Italian styles. After visiting Naples, Bruegel stayed for an extended period in Rome, where he established a friendship, or at the very least a collaboration, with the miniaturist Giulio Clovio. He later passed through the Alps, which greatly stimulated his imagination, as is attested to by numerous drawings, and the memory of this sight remained with him all his life. As Van Mander cleverly put it, "It was said that traveling through the Alps he had swallowed mountains and rocks, which upon his return he spit back out onto canvases and panels." Using such works of art, it is possible to reconstruct Bruegel's return journey, through the Ticino Valley, San Gottardo, and from there to the Grigioni and perhaps the Tyrol.

Two letters from the Bolognese geographer Scipio Fabius to his colleague Ortelius concern Bruegel's Italian trip: one, from 1561, asks for news of "our dearest Petrus Bruochl," and the other, from 1563, sends regards to both Bruegel and Marten de Vos, who apparently was Bruegel's companion on at least part of the journey.

Upon his return to Antwerp, Bruegel established a close collaboration with Hierony-mus Cock (1510–1570), an extremely active editor, bookseller, and print merchant, who had a shop, "In de Vier Winden" ("To the Four Winds"), a name which clearly expressed Cock's ambitions. His shop was an emporium of European art, a meeting place for intellectuals, a cultural center of the city. The tireless Bruegel provided drawings to be engraved and circulated in the form of prints by Cock, whom Vasari mentioned in glowing terms: "Hieronymus Cock, whom I met in Rome while I was in the service of Cardinal Ippolito de' Medici." Of Cock's skill as an engraver Vasari said, referring to certain prints, that "they were engraved by Hieronymus Cock, whose hand is proud, sure, and very vigorous."

Bruegel stayed in Antwerp for ten years, leaving only for a brief trip to Amsterdam in 1662, which is documented by drawings (now in Besançon) of the fortifications, towers, and gates of that city. In 1563 Bruegel married his first teacher's daughter, Mayken Coecke (Van Mander wrote that Bruegel had carried her as a baby in his arms when he was an apprentice in her father's shop), and moved to Brussels; their marriage is recorded in the register of the church of Notre-Dame-de-la-Chapelle: "Peeter Brugel/solmt/Maryken Cocks."

There has been much discussion of why Bruegel decided to move from Antwerp. According to Van Mander, the move was caused by Coecke's widow, who ran an art business in Brussels; she had also published her husband's posthumous work, *Moeurs et Fachons de faire de Turcsz*. Bruegel's mother-in-law prompted the move in order to force Pieter to break off with a servant woman with whom he was living in Antwerp, but, apart from these domestic reasons for the move, many scholars feel that

Bruegel was compelled to leave Antwerp because of the political danger that his intimacy with humanists and freethinkers placed him in, as we shall see further on.

The few short years (not more than six) that Bruegel spent in Brussels were blessed with an intense artistic activity which produced his greatest masterpieces. According to Van Mander, the city of Brussels commissioned from Bruegel a series of paintings illustrating the work on the canal between Brussels and Antwerp — a commission that was canceled by the artist's untimely death in September 1569. Bruegel was buried in the same church where six years earlier he had been married, and where his son Jan built a monument to him which was renovated in 1676 by his distant descendant David Tenier. The monument reads, PETRO BREUGELIO/EXACTISSIMAE INDUSTRIAE/ ARTIS VENUSTISSIMAE/PICTORI, and was decorated with a canvas by Rubens, *Christ Giving the Keys of the Church to St. Peter,* almost as if to allude to the skill of the painter who had unlocked people's eyes to the world's beauty.

Regarding Bruegel's character, once again we must turn to Van Mander (in addition to the painter's works), who wrote that "he was a calm, wise person, a man of few words; but in the company of his friends he was amusing, and he loved to frighten his friends and apprentices with stories of ghosts and a thousand other devilries. . . ." In fact, two of Bruegel's favorite motifs were humorous pieces and "devilries" à la Bosch; this predilection earned him the nickname of "Piet den Drol," Pieter the Clown. As far as his apprentices go, we unfortunately have absolutely no information about how Bruegel's studio was organized, or even whether he really had one, which is not at all certain.

There is no authentic portrait of Bruegel; his ironic drawing of *The Painter and the Connoisseur* is perhaps a self-portrait. The profile published by Lampsonius in his *Pictorum aliquot celebrium Germaniae inferioris effigies* (Antwerp, 1572), which depicts the artist with a long flowing beard, is another possible genuine likeness. The serious-looking bearded man speaking to a monk on the extreme right of *The Wedding Banquet* is considered to be a self-portrait, as is a similar figure in the crowd of *The Preaching of St. John the Baptist.*

Bruegel had two sons, both painters: Pieter II (born in 1564), who was called "The Infernal Bruegel" because of the frequency of fiery backgrounds in his paintings, and who specialized in making accurate copies of his father's pictures; and Jan (1568–1625), called "The Velvet Bruegel" (perhaps because he had a predilection for refined fabrics), who was active in Italy (he knew Federico Borromeo, and several of his paintings are in the Ambrosian Library in Milan) and specialized in flowers and animals seen with a miniaturist's scientific detail; Jan frequently collaborated with Rubens.

Pieter Bruegel was held in high esteem by his contemporaries. His friend Abraham Ortelius wrote of him in his *Album Amicorum:* "No one, except for the jealous, the envious, or those who know nothing of painting, no one can deny that Pieter Bruegel was the most perfect painter of his time." Great collectors and patrons sought to obtain his works; the wealthy Niclaes Jongelinck of Antwerp commissioned *The Months* from Bruegel and possessed no less than sixteen of his works. Rubens owned a dozen paintings by Bruegel;[1] the curator of the poor of

[1] List of paintings found in the house where the late Peter Paul Rubens, *Chevalier,* died, 1640.

View of Reggio Calabria
Rotterdam, Boymans-van Beuningen Museum

Antwerp, Pieter Stevens (1668), owned eleven. Cardinal Perrenot de Granville, a collector and patron of Bruegel,[2] violently protested the disappearance of his Bruegels in the sack of Mechlin and asked the canon Morillon to find a way to get them back or get others. Morillon responded (December 9, 1572), "If you mean to re-acquire works by Bruegel, you should know that they are very expensive; now that he is dead they are even more in demand than before, and sell for fifty, one hundred, and two hundred écus." Federico Borromeo, too, wanted to obtain a painting by Bruegel and requested one from the painter's son Jan, who replied in a letter (1609) that there were no more to be had, since Emperor Rudolph had snatched them all up; Jan made Rubens a gift of a grisaille by his father in his own collection, *Christ and the Adultress* (now in the Seilern Collection in London). Even before this time, the Archduke Ernest, who was governor of the Low Countries from 1591 to 1595, had been an avid collector of works by Bruegel (he bought the *Wedding Banquet* for one hundred and fifty florins); at his death his collection passed to Emperor Rudolph. Despite the sack by the Swedes and the works stolen from Prague in 1648, the largest collection of paintings by Bruegel is in Vienna, thanks to the Hapsburgs' assiduous acquisitions.

Bruegel remained very popular until the beginning of the seventeenth century, when for various reasons his fame began to diminish — first and foremost because he came to be labeled as a merely amusing painter who imitated Bosch. Already before Bruegel's death, Guicciardini had written in his previously mentioned *Description of All the Low Countries:* "Pieter Bruegel of Breda

[2]Inventory of the furniture of Granvelle house, 1607.

is a great imitator of the art and fantasy of Hieronymus Bosch, whence he has acquired the nickname of Hieronymus Bosch II." Lampsonius, in the verses that accompany the portrait of Bruegel mentioned before, wrote: "Who is this new Bosch?" and praised Bruegel for having renewed both Bosch's humor and bitterness. Van Mander affirmed that "the works of Hieronymus Bosch were his particular object of study, and he painted many 'diabolical' and comical works, earning himself the nickname of 'Piet den Drol,' that is, Pieter the Clown." And so on, up to Baudelaire's famous remarks (1857), but it is highly likely that the French poet was referring as much to Bosch as he was to Bruegel when he called him a playful, amusing painter of the common people. Van Mander wrote that "one can look at few of his works without laughing."

This lesser fame, which lasted a long time, was certainly not based on Bruegel's paintings, which were jealously conserved by his friends and collectors, but rather on his drawings, which are strongly reminiscent of Bosch, and which were widely known due to the prints Cock made of them.

Bruegel did not again receive fair critical treatment until the end of the nineteenth century. One of his most acute critics, Dvořak, wrote: "It is certainly an error to consider Bruegel as merely a continuation of Bosch," just as it was mistaken to consider him as having come from the world of the peasants he so often depicted. Instead, he should be seen as the dispassionate yet sympathetic artist who painted rustic scenes in which he expressed his views of man and the world.

But here we run into another one of the obstacles which have always created problems for those who study Bruegel: the search for the philosophy behind his art. This brings to mind a comment by Ortelius, who claimed that in Bruegel's works there was always more thought than painting. Too many critics have become bogged down in trying to discover the meaning of Bruegel's works, his philosophical position, his political allusions, and so on. As the perceptive critic Grossmann has put it, "The interpretation of Bruegel's symbolism and the search for the meaning of his works have been the main object of the studies of this artist during the last forty years." And all this has been at the expense of what really counts — Bruegel's amazing personal modes of expression. Friedlander writes with an ironic smile that "Bruegel was definitely less complicated than his critics, but much smarter."

When the young Bruegel returned to his native country, Antwerp was in the full flower of her prosperity, Bruges having lost her crucial position after the Zwijn canal, which had connected her to the sea, became unnavigable. The vast port of Antwerp (which Dürer had drawn in 1520) in the Scheldt estuary was the most important in Europe; a Venetian ambassador complained that Antwerp had overshadowed Venice, while an English diplomat declared her to be "one of the wonders of the world." With the discovery of America and the circumnavigation of Africa, the world's maritime center had shifted; Antwerp had become a huge international marketplace. Guicciardini called Antwerp "the common homeland of all Christian nations" and affirmed that one could learn the ways and customs of half the countries in the world there. From everywhere came merchants and bankers (for example, the powerful Fuggers); Antwerp was full of warehouses and marketplaces, and was a center for im-

portation of goods from every part of the world, especially wines, grains, and textiles, local products, and woven rugs and tapestries. The city had a bourgeois character (in contrast to the aristocratic atmosphere of Brussels, which was the seat of the government and of the nobility); its life was festive and turbulent. In 1560 there were 150,000 inhabitants, 360 of which were artists, compared to only 169 bakers and 78 butchers. Antwerp was the center of an extremely active art market; many exhibits were held in Kerplaats, and even modest middle-class homes could boast paintings and prints.[3] Thus Antwerp was not only a commercial center but also an important cultural center, with a vast number of printers (the most important of which was Plantin), editors, and booksellers, and a large traffic in prints and paintings.

Naturally, one of the results of such an intense commercial traffic was a rich artistic and cultural exchange. Flemish artists such as Roger Van der Weyden and Justus of Ghent visited Italy, while Italians such as Antonello da Messina and the previously mentioned engraver Ghisi visited Flanders. Works, too, traveled, such as the magnificent *Portinari Altar-piece* by Hugo Van der Goes in Florence, and paintings by Flemish artists in Genoa and Sicily; a Madonna by Michelangelo made its way to Bruges. During the sixteenth century the fascination of the Italian Renaissance caused an invasion of Flemish artists in Italy, among whom were Bruegel's first teacher Pieter Coecke and his patron Hieronymus Cock. Yet we must repeat that Bruegel remained impervious to this rage for Italian art. "Italy for

[3] A testimony to the wealth and splendor of the painter's guild in Antwerp can be found in Dürer's diary (August 5, 1520) when he was solemnly welcomed by his Flemish colleagues.

him was essentially another landscape" (Philippot).

Antwerp, with so many people of different races and religions, enjoyed a moral climate of great tolerance, favorable to liberal and progressive ideas and therefore also to the Protestant Reformation. Charles V had made every effort to thwart and repress these tendencies with the famous edicts threatening Lutherans and Anabaptists with atrocious punishments. Even if they renounced their heresy they were punished (men decapitated, women buried alive); if they persisted, they were condemned to be burned at the stake. Tens of thousands of Anabaptists perished in this way. When Philip II succeeded his father, he was even harsher. He left his sister Margaret of Parma as regent of the Low Countries, assisted by Cardinal Perrenot of Granvelle, a bitter enemy of the nobility and of their traditional privileges. In an atmosphere of suspicion, betrayal, oppression, and inquisition, the "Nobles' Compromise" (which also included Catholics) succeeded in removing the cardinal (1564) and suppressing the edicts and the Inquisition. The city's prosperity began to decline, many nobles and artisans emigrated, and there were great poverty, famine, and unemployment. For quite some time Lutheran preachers had been holding secret meetings and had found many followers, especially from the men of the working classes, such as laborers, artisans, and weavers. In August 1566 an insurrection exploded; the iconoclasts destroyed works of art and devastated churches and convents. The rebellion was quelled, but Philip II still sent a powerful army led by the Duke of Alba, which crossed the Alps and reached Flanders in August 1567. There followed a bloody series of arrests and executions in which the leaders of the insurrection, the Counts of Egmont and Horne, perished along with many other nobles.

Let us now return to Bruegel and his years in Antwerp, and try to find a correlation between the political and economic conditions which we have briefly discussed and his works. Obviously Antwerp must have made a substantial contribution to Bruegel's artistic development, not only in regard to the drawings he produced to be made into prints in the workshop "In den Vier Winden," but also because of the generosity of the collectors who bought his works.

As far as the political situation of the times, it is difficult to see how it is reflected in Bruegel's works, as many critics have obstinately tried to do. It is highly likely that there are allusions to the torments of the Inquisition in the gloomy background of *The Triumph of Death*. We can also be fairly certain that a clandestine Protestant sermon heard in the country inspired the canvas of *The Preaching of John the Baptist* to a crowd of listeners. But the theories that *The Conversion of St. Paul* is related to the Duke of Alba crossing the Alps or that the violence perpetrated by the Duke is reflected in *The Massacre of the Innocents* are not very probable, for reasons of chronology, and also taking into account Bruegel's prudent, retiring character. "He was a discerning man of uncommon intelligence" — writes a recent critic, Marijnissen — "certainly he had a sharp critical spirit, but we should take care not to make him out to be a Marxist freethinker."

It seems more than likely that in the circle of humanists and libertines who frequented Cock's shop Bruegel used his ears more than his tongue, probably sharing in his heart of hearts their exaltation of freedom

18

and tolerance, their invectives against tyranny and the Inquisition, and their admiration for the progress of the human spirit (this was also the century of Copernicus, Montaigne, and Galileo). These humanists were closely watched by the mistrustful politicians, who saw them as cunning advocates of reform and admirers of Erasmus (all of whose works had been placed on the Index by the Council of Trent in 1546), whose skepticism they viewed as extremely dangerous. This was the atmosphere of suspicion that surrounded the group of humanists and men of culture of which the artist had become a part, and the prudent Bruegel was aware of the storm that was about to break over their heads. Already in 1562 the printer Plantin had left Antwerp on the pretext of business; he had printed unorthodox books and was a member of a heretical sect, the *Schola Caritas* of Herri Niclaes (of which De Tolnay erroneously believes Bruegel was also a member). Ortelius, who was suspected of being sympathetic to the Reformation, had gone into exile in London. In 1567 the humanist, theologian, and translator of the classics, Dirk Coornhert (who claimed to be a Catholic but not a Papist), was arrested and sent into exile, a very frequent occurrence. In fact, it is estimated that in that year eighty-seven percent of the foreigners in London were Flemish exiles.

This situation was in all likelihood the serious reason for Bruegel's decision to move to Brussels (as Jedlicka has pointed out), leaving behind the city he knew so well and his patrons and friends like Frankert, who had been his companion on outings to the country. And this move must surely have taken its toll on the peace-loving Bruegel, who saw himself compelled to find a new life with his young wife and children. Bruegel doesn't seem to have formed new friendships in Brussels (except perhaps with the sculptor Jongelinck, his patron's brother, who had a studio in Cardinal Perrenot's palace). The years Bruegel spent in Brussels were of a retiring life-style and intense artistic activity, which produced the prudent painter's greatest masterpieces.

View of Waltersspurg
Brunswick, Bowdoin College Museum of Art

The Works of Bruegel the Elder

Before his trip to Italy the young Bruegel must have devoted himself primarily to drawing; he was probably introduced to the techniques of miniature and tempera on canvas by Coecke's wife Mayken, who was a native of Mechlin, where the medium of tempera on canvas was widespread. A recently published document (1964) proves the young artist's collaboration on an altar-piece for the glovemakers' guild in the church of San Rambont in Mechlin, the central part of which was by Pieter Baltens, and the side panels in grisaille by Bruegel; none of this work has survived.

Bruegel's familiarity with the art of miniature is demonstrated by his collaboration with Clovio in Rome. The document published by Bertolotti (1882) refers to various works by the young Flemish artist, in Clovio's possession: "An ivory tower of Babel by the hand of Master Pieter Bruegel . . . A gouache painting of a tree by Master Pieter Bruegel . . . A gouache picture of Leo of France by the hand of Master Pieter Bruegel," and other works — drawings and prints; but above all "a miniature half by his (that is, Clovio's) hand, the other by Master Pieter Bruegel." The indefatigable De Tolnay has found possible evidence of Bruegel's hand in an illustration of the Towneley Lesson-book (fo. 21, Public Library, New York), as he stated in an article in the *Burlington Magazine* in 1965. The page is covered by a *Last Judgement* by Clovio in an elaborate framework, in a corner of which, in a different style, are ships on a stormy sea, and in the background, a city in flames whose inhabitants are fleeing. In this miniscule depiction (40 × 70 mm), De Tolnay points out Bruegel's collaboration with Clovio and his training in the art of the miniature (which can also be seen in some of his later works, such as *The Suicide of Saul* and *The Conversion of St. Paul*).

However, the greater part of Bruegel's activity in Italy is represented by numerous beautiful drawings, on the basis of which it is possible to form a rough, partial idea of his itinerary. There is a pen drawing from 1553 of a *View of Reggio Calabria*. An engraving (executed by F. Huys, with the inscription "Bruegel inven.") depicts a *Naval Battle in the Strait of Messina* (on the basis of which Burchard has attributed *The Port of Naples* to Bruegel). From Bruegel's stay in Rome we have a drawing of *The Banks of the Tiber* (with an apocryphal signature), a *Prospectus Tyburtinus* based on a drawing by Bruegel and printed by Cock, and two prints of *River Landscapes* with tiny mythological figures, Icarus and Psyche, with the inscription "Br. inv. Romae 1553."

There was a precise memory of Bruegel's Alpine passage in a lost work listed among Rubens' possessions: "Mont San Gotard by Bruegel the Elder"; another precise topographical reference to the Alps is to be found in the drawing designated *Waltersspurg,* which can be identified as Waltensburg in the Rhine Valley.

Bruegel's early activity was primarily graphic, and for his entire life he tirelessly provided Cock with drawings of a moral character, illustrations of proverbs, satirical drawings, and "devilries" à la Bosch, which were then circulated in the form of prints. In his last years in Brussels this activity slowed down considerably.

Before going on to examine Bruegel's paintings, we would like to discuss briefly his original drawings.

From Bruegel's memory of the Alpine landscape derive the twelve *Large Landscapes* with small human figures, such as *The Penitent Magdalen, St. Jerome,* etc. This series was published by Cock from 1553 to 1555. Bruegel's collaboration with this editor was intense: in 1558 Cock published the series of *The Capital Sins,* which are strongly reminiscent of Bosch; the following series, *The Seven Virtues* (1560), have a more personal flavor, less dependent on Bosch's style. In fact, Bosch was so popular at this time that Cock did not hesitate to put his name under the engraving *Big Fish Eat Little Ones* made from an autograph drawing by

Bruegel in 1556. Another series of prints made from drawings by Bruegel is that of the *Sea Vessels,* engraved by F. Huys, which as we have said reveal the artist's knowledge of and passion for ships, and tend to confirm the theory that he traveled by sea from Marseilles to Calabria. From the large number of prints made from drawings by Bruegel, there is only one etching by his own hand, the *Landscape with a Rabbit Hunter* of 1566, which according to specialists reveals a fairly clumsy use of the engraver's burin.

Leaving behind the engravings, we will now glance at Bruegel's autograph drawings of a relatively late date. *Summer* (1563) and *Spring* (1565) were intended to be part of a suite of *The Four Seasons,* which was completed by Hans Bol. Particularly noteworthy are *The Beekeepers* (1568), the *Two Blind Men and a Peasant Woman* (1562), and the famous ironic drawing of *The Painter and the Connoisseur* (circa 1565), considered by some critics to be a self-portrait. A unique example of Bruegel's graphic work is a woodcut ready for the engraver, *The Disheveled Bride* (New York, Metropolitan Museum), in which a couple dances before a torn curtain, a motif which also appears in *The Battle between Carnival and Lent.*

The well-known and interesting series of drawings of real people, *naer het leven* ("from life") — peasants and townspeople often seen from the rear, drawn with a sure hand, with annotations on colors — has been attributed to Bruegel, with certain reservations, reservations which are strengthened by the fact that none of these figures are found in Bruegel's paintings. Recently, two scholars, F. V. Leeuwen and J. A. Spicer, have attributed these drawings to the Flemish artist Roeland Savery (1576–1639).

Prospectus Tyburtinus
engraving

Bruegel's first painting — since we have only documentary evidence of the Mechlin altarpiece — can be considered as being the aforementioned miniature in the Towneley Lesson-book, to which a small panel, brought to light by Grossmann, the *Landscape with Ships and City in Flames* (which that scholar dates about 1552 to 1553), is related. The *Landscape with the Calling of the Apostles* is signed and dated 1553; it has been suggested that the small human figures are by Marten de Vos, Bruegel's traveling companion in Italy. The next signed and dated work by Bruegel is from 1557, the *Landscape with Sower* (Plate 1), which, like Bruegel's preceding works, is in keeping with the local tradition of Patenier (a landscape artist whom Dürer praised) and Herri Met de Bles (called Civetta). Here Bruegel depicts a vast composite landscape, seen cartographically from above. The work is traditional even from a chromatic point of view, with its brown foreground, green central portion, and blue background, with subtle shadings and mixtures that give the whole an air of solemnity. The spectator's eye is led from the foreground (at the left of which is the figure of the sower) to the river which spreads beneath the distant mountains and finally becomes one with the luminous sky. As far as the Biblical parable (Matt. 12:3) goes, the critics who occupy themselves with trying to discover Bruegel's "philosophy" see the fact that the birds are pecking the seeds as a symbol of the uselessness of human action, and therefore an early expression of Bruegel's pessimism. But if this excessively subtle argument were valid, that pessimism would also have to be attributed to St. Matthew, and ultimately to Christ himself.

It is essential to note that Bruegel's activity primarily as a painter began in 1559 and therefore lasted barely a decade. The difficult analysis of his pictures is to some degree aided by the fact that almost all of them are dated. But we will begin our analysis with the examination of two undated works which have been the object of much controversy, not only on account of their dates but also their attributions.

The painting of *The Port of Naples* (Plate 2) marks a definite stop on Bruegel's Italian trip. The attribution of this work to Bruegel has been generally accepted by scholars, but its date has not been so easily agreed upon. Friedlander dates it 1558, and Grossmann considers it to be a late work, whereas Jedlika instead dates it around 1555 to 1556 (except for the miniaturistic treatment of the waves, this seems to us to be the most plausible date for this work).

This painting's faithfulness to reality — an almost unique occurrence in Bruegel's work — is indisputable: we can see Castel dell'Uovo, Castel Nuovo, Sant'Elmo, etc.; the one departure from reality is the depiction of the jetty as curved rather than rectangular. However, this departure is justifiable for reasons of composition—that is, in order to continue the curved motion from left to right of the ships, a motion that is emphasized by the sky, which is clear on the left and cloudy on the right, and the wind, which fills the sails of the ships and ripples the sea with thin waves capped with white foam (whose minute treatment, as we have mentioned, brings to mind Bruegel's early training in the art of miniature).

This is perhaps the picture which appears in the previously cited Granvelle Inventory of 1607, "Ships on a calm sea with small figures and a distant landscape, by Pieter Bruegel," and in the Rubens inventory of 1640, "A piece representing small ships done in tempera, by the said Bruegel the

Elder." But whether both of these descriptions are of the same painting, and whether that painting was *The Port of Naples,* is impossible to ascertain.

At any rate, we should note here that this painting is proof of Bruegel's love of the sea and his knowledge of maritime activity.

Another beautiful sailing ship is depicted in *The Fall of Icarus* (Plate 3), which is one of Bruegel's best-known works, and one which has caused a great divergence of opinion among critics. There are two known versions of this work: this one, in Brussels, and one in the Von Buuren Collection in New York. The two works present certain differences in their details: in this version there is no indication of Dedalus, who appears in the Von Buuren version; in the New York painting the sun is high, while in this one it is almost sunset. Jedlika believes these two works to be copies of a lost original; Glück, instead, believes they are both originals. The date, too, has been a subject for dispute; some scholars date the works 1555, while others feel it to be a very late work.

At any rate, this is an enchanting image, flooded with light over the sea. Its subject is taken from Ovid's *Metamorphoses* (VIII, 217–233). The plowman in the foreground continues peacefully to make his furrows; the fisherman is intent on his line and doesn't see the legs and hand ringed with foam sinking into the sea; the shepherd looks up, perhaps to suggest the presence of Dedalus. Leaving aside the magical interpretation of this work (Van Lennep), we should note that the head of a cadaver is sticking out of the bushes above the horse's head; this work is in all likelihood a curious mixture of classical and popular cultures. In fact, there is a proverb that says: "The plow does not stop for the death of a man" — the world goes on; it stops neither for the death of an anonymous man nor for that of a famous mythological character. This magnificent fable of light and color has inspired many different interpretations: some have seen it as a depiction of the Strait of Messina; others more recently have identified it with Lake Verbano seen from Ronco above Ascona (where Bruegel probably passed through on his return trip from Italy). But these tangents take away from the appreciation of the picture's beauty.

Bruegel turned to popular culture once again in his first large picture, signed and dated 1559 — the painting of *Flemish Proverbs,* which appears in the Stevens inventory of 1668 with the title, "The world upside down, represented by various Proverbs and Morals." Symbols of this "upside-down world" in fact are the overturned globe under the window on the left or the woman in red in the central proverb putting a blue cape on her husband, a sign of her unfaithfulness. These one hundred twenty proverbs or sayings have been fully explained by W. Fraenger (1923), and more recently by Marijnissen, and constitute a sort of encyclopedia of popular Flemish sayings. The composition consists of a crowd of figures placed within an architectural setting on the left and the sea on the right, following a diagonal which acts as the backbone of the composition. This painting is of interest not only for its folkloristic content but also for its affinity with Erasmus' *Adages* and the proverbs which embellish Rabelais' lively pages.

Critics have attempted to see a pessimistic outlook on Bruegel's part in this panorama of popular wisdom (or ignorance), but this interpretation is rather forced. Rather, what we have here are sayings which become funny or odd because they have been concretely depicted. They are images created by the common people (Flemish or of any other country); in fact, one could make a long list of them: ''Take the bread from one's mouth,'' ''Close the stall after the oxen have escaped,'' and so on. It is difficult to see what a pessimistic view of life could have to do with all this.

Some of the other proverbs depicted here are: on the left, in the foreground, a woman tying the devil to a cushion signifies feminine evil (this image returns in *Dulle Griet);* the man gnawing on a column directly in back of her symbolizes bigotry; another figure illustrates, ''Don't butt your head against a wall''; the two men shearing a sheep and a pig represent riches and poverty; another man tries to ''block up the well after the calf is drowned''; the man inside the glass globe signifies that one must know how to bend or adapt in this world (the image recurs in *The Misanthrope);* the dandy balancing the globe on his thumb has his way with everyone; and so on. On the roof at the left the cakes symbolize abundance (as in *The Land of Cockaigne).*

What is important to note here is Bruegel's constant interest in folk proverbs, which is a continuous vein in his works, even in his very last painting, the *Storm at Sea* (Plate 40). In fact two opposite poles can be individualized in Bruegel's works: his sympathy for the rustic life and his relations with intellectuals and humanists. From these contrasting elements is born, in part, the fascination of Bruegel's universe — all of this, of course, over and above the absolute value of his work, that is, its beauty, which is a fantastic, poetic creation of a singular attractiveness.

Even more thronged with minute figures is *The Battle between Carnival and Lent* (Plate 5), from the same year, 1559. In a view seen from above, Bruegel depicts a large square bounded by inns on the left and a church on the right, with the crowd divided into two opposing factions; a compositional diagonal acts as a line of demarcation (Faggin has industriously diagramed this composition). The ''leaders'' of the two factions meet in the center foreground: the fat Carnival, astride a barrel, brandishes a spit loaded with food; Lent, a skeletal old woman with a beehive on her head, holding a long baker's shovel with two herrings on it, sits on a cart pulled by a monk and a nun.

Grotesque masked figures follow the King of Carnival, enjoying sinful pleasures: gluttony, lust, gambling, acting out rustic pantomimes. At the left is the fable of *The Disheveled Bride* who dances before a tent; in the background is the fable of Orsone and Valentino. In the midst of the unheeding crowd is a group of cripples, one of whom wears a fox's tail on his cape. Behind, the starving Lent people are doing good works, distributing alms, helping the needy, leading the blind, burying the dead (one of whom was in the cart being pulled by two old women). The faithful leave the church carrying chairs; beside the well is the fish seller's stand. The colorful, mobile crowd is animated by children playing with a top, chasing each other, doing a round dance. The diverse, multicolored little figures stand out against the scorched background of the square.

An entire painting dating from the following year (1560) is devoted to *Children's Games* (Plate 6). This picture is swarming with tiny figures who amuse themselves at eighty-four different games. The background is formed by a building, to the left of which the view opens out on trees and a river, while on the right a perspective

The Banks of the Tiber
Chatsworth, Devonshire Collection

view of a long street draws the spectator's eye into the distance (this is possibly a reflection of Serlio's illustrations as published by Coecke). A good portion of the games are universally known — hoops, marbles, bowls, stilts; others are imitations of grown-ups — a wedding march, baptism, shop, etc.; others are less common. In the dark open doorway of the house at the rear a girl balances a broom in her hand; another little girl, having left off playing for a moment, calmly urinates, framed by the exterior arch of the house.

The play of colors is lively here, as is the rhythm which scatters and unites the figures of the children, which seen separately are not terribly mobile, muffled up as they are in adult clothing, with their round faces and inexpressive eyes. Stridbeck's observation that this swarming mass should be seen as an allegory for the insane, sinful world is rather strange; Salvini, as well, insists "that, in fact, these infantile games are an allegory for man's absurd and vain struggles is clear."

This gay assembly of playing children, from which adults are strictly excluded, recalls the list of no less than two hundred fifteen games that varied Gargantua's day; in fact, on many occasions Bruegel seems to be a kindred spirit to Rabelais.

There are no works by Bruegel dated 1561. We have three from the following two years, of a decidedly "Boschian" flavor — *The Triumph of Death, The Expulsion of the Rebellious Angels,* and *Dulle Griet.*

The apocalyptic vision of *The Triumph of Death* (Plate 7) is a sadistic, wanton depiction of horror worthy of a painter in love with life and therefore even more sensitive to the terror of death. On a sterile and barren terrain (whose only flora are the gallows and tall wheels against the sky, where smoke and flames remind one of the gas chambers and crematoriums of recent history) the witches' sabbath of death takes place — death which triumphs over and annihilates humanity in a ghastly accumulation of details. In the foreground appears the medieval theme of the macabre dance, representing the equality of death. On the far left, a skeleton shows an hourglass, whose sands have run out, to a king, arrayed in his crown, mantle, and armor and holding a sceptre, while another skeleton dips his hands into a barrel of gold coins. A slumping cardinal (dressed in green!) is held up by another skeleton; a dead mother holding a distaff clutches her still living baby; a pilgrim with his knapsack and staff has his throat cut; a soldier lies slain while his companion tries to defend himself; a clown is hiding himself under the tablecloth on the right while a masked demon overturns card tables, flasks, and playing cards; and finally on the far right a pair of lovers are absorbed in song, while Death accompanies them on the viola.

Behind this dance of death the unruly crowd of the living is being urged into Death's trap (from the crowd emerges a fragile female nude, the only one in all of Bruegel's paintings), along with skeletal horses, skeletons wrapped in white shrouds, and cartloads of skulls, in an endless series of ghastly details such as cadavers hanging from gallows and a skeleton decapitating a man at the foot of a pole whose wheel is occupied by human remains.

There is no necessity to suppose, as some critics have, that a work seen by Bruegel in Palazzo Scalfani in Palermo inspired this work, which is extremely original; Bruegel's imagination had no need for external stimuli or suggestions. Friedländer

The Penitent Magdalen
engraving

has rightly observed that in this desperate representation the concept of a Christian death is totally lacking: nowhere do we see a consoling priest or a sign of faith in the afterlife. Death here is seen as a definitive annihilation.

The influence of Bosch is evident in *The Expulsion of the Rebellious Angels* (Plate 8), as well as an echo of the fifteenth century in the angels with long trumpets and Gothic cloaks, and the lean figure of the Archangel Michael, who seems to have come from a Romanesque tympanum at Autun (as has been suggested). Against a background which is perhaps too brightly lit by the sun is a screaming mass of monstrous creatures: toads, fish, snakes, lizards, huge butterflies, abominations — all the ghastly horrors of Bosch, certainly without his mysterious and disquieting magic, but with an enchanting chromatic richness in the glimmering colors against the dark red of the lower portion.

Here more than ever we can see the abyss between Bruegel's art and that of Romanist or Italianate artists such as Frans Floris, who had painted the same subject eight years earlier. Floris, who had been in Rome for the unveiling of Michelangelo's *Last Judgement,* painted monstrous Boschian heads on a heap of disjointed anatomies, with eloquent incongruence, while in Bruegel's work the lesson of Bosch is perfectly assimilated by an artist who remains autonomous even when he openly imitates. Bruegel had companions in his resistance to the rage for Italian art, in artists such as Pieters Aertsen and Joakim Buekelaer, painters of realistic genre scenes, still lifes, marketplaces, and kitchens; however, Bruegel's work was a far cry from the popularesque naturalism of these artists.

But the painting by Bruegel that is closest to Bosch is *Dulle Griet* ("Mad Meg") (Plate 9), which is inhabited by all of Bosch's flora and fauna: eggs, trees, cordages, fish, and lyre-birds, against a background of smoke and flames. This is a teaming anthology of Boschian nightmarish inventions, dominated by the shouting figure of Dulle Griet, a raging hag who, in armor and a helmet, her sword drawn, runs into the mouth of Hell: half fortress, half scaly fish, with its mouth wide open, into which a river runs. But who is this hag or fury, and what does she represent? She is a universally known creature, Mad Meg or Margot la Folle or Roaring Meg, whose name appears on cannons in Ghent and Scotland, and is generally interpreted as a symbol of greed or avarice and a summation of the capital sins which Bruegel had illustrated in a series of prints four years earlier. She carries various objects — an apron, a basket, and a frying pan, household items and a little jewel box. A small figure of a woman behind her is tying the devil to a cushion (a motif we have already seen in the *Flemish Proverbs*), signifying that feminine slyness and perfidy can even defeat the devil. Above an unruly group of women rises a disquieting invention: a creature which has a boat on its back, with a crystal sphere, and is digging out gold from the egg in its posterior to spur on the swarm of women fighting to get at it. This disturbing nightmare is full of inventions which tend to make one disregard the refined beauty of the picture, as seen, for example, in the red velvet of Meg's sleeves or the reflections from her armor.

These early paintings by Bruegel are more to be read, that is, to be examined and enjoyed at close range, rather than seen as a whole, for their composition or chromatic harmony. The spectator's eye is attracted by

Big Fish Eat Little Ones
Vienna, Albertina

the innumerable details and by the dazzling inventions in *Dulle Griet, The Expulsion of the Rebellious Angels,* and *The Triumph of Death.* And these paintings are the ones which illustrators of Bruegel's works have concentrated upon, reproducing details which help us to penetrate deeper into the artist's world. Particularly noteworthy is Marijnissen and Seidel's splendidly illustrated volume.

Bruegel's first paintings, which constitute a "revival" of Bosch, must have been a sort of spiritual purge for the artist (unless they were specifically commissioned, which is not at all improbable). At any rate, from this time on all traces of Bosch's disquieting world disappear from Bruegel's works.

We next encounter a highly refined little picture of *Two Monkeys* (Plate 10) in an arched window, through which we are shown the evanescent outline of the city of Antwerp. Some critics have read political allusions into this painting, allusions to the servitude of the Flemish provinces; others have found a moral significance, that of man as fettered by sin. But it is much more likely that this is simply a study of two chained animals, two African Monkeys (redheaded *Colobidae*), who interested the painter with their soft brown fur and red heads. Bruegel frames them in the curve of the arch, playing on the curves of their backs and tails, participating in their silent, inquisitive sadness.

One is tempted to say that there is less participation on the painter's part in the *Old Woman* (Plate 11), whose attribution to Bruegel is now universal and whose date has been subject to controversy. At any rate, it is a noteworthy piece of "portraiture," which is a genre completely absent from Bruegel's work. In fact, it is surprising that no portrait by Bruegel exists, of any of

his many Erasmian friends in Antwerp, of his friend Franckert, etc., while we have Rubens' portrait of Ortelius and Moro's portrait of Granvelle.

But one should note that up to the end of his brief career Bruegel often depicted people from the back or with their faces covered, avoiding the face and any personal expression, as if he were interested in portraying not the individual but rather the universal, generic man.

The small panel with *The Suicide of Saul* (Plate 12), of unusually reduced pictorial proportions, is based on the Biblical text (Kings I:31) describing a battle between the Jews and the Philistines. With defeat imminent and his three sons dead, "Saul said to his armor bearer: 'Draw thy sword, and kill me, lest these uncircumcised come, and slay me, and mock at me.' And his armor bearer would not, for he was struck with exceeding great fear. Then Saul took his sword, and fell upon it. And when his armor bearer saw this, to wit, he also fell upon his sword and died with him." This episode is an example of punishment for the sin of pride and also appears in Dante (*Purgatory* XII, 40):

O Saul! how dead you appeared
on your sword in Gilboa...

The scene of the suicide here is minute and isolated on a rocky plateau in the left foreground; of much more interest is the magnificent scene of steep gorges and precipices among dark fir groves (another memory of Bruegel's trip through the Alps), in which soldiers appear like ants, and their lances like pins. Scholars have rightly connected this miniaturistic treatment to Altdorfer's *Battle of Isso* (1529) and to Bruegel's early training under Coecke's wife. In the distance are a calm river and a far-off city.

The Flight into Egypt is the only surviving work from the aforementioned Granvelle inventory (Besançon, 1607): ''Landscape of the Madonna going to Egypt, by Bruegel the Elder,'' with indications of the proportions which correspond to those of the existing picture, taking into account that they include the frame ''with its gold molding.'' As the inventory indicates, this work is above all a vast cosmic landscape (*Weltlandschaft*) seen from above, with on the left rocky mountains and on the right a large river between eroded banks. The fleeing figures, seen from behind, play a very small part in this landscape, which includes a broken idol, an element taken from an apocryphal Gospel. The red of the Virgin's clothing forms a bright spot of color in the beautiful landscape, which Grossmann feels is an anticipation of Rubens. Extreme attention is paid even to the most minor natural details: the bird on the willow tree and the grass — as in the marvellous thistle in *The Way to Calvary* or the iris in *The Blind Leading the Blind*. These details have a naturalist's precision, but more than that they possess a poet's power of transfiguration. This is an extremely significant aspect of Bruegel's art, and a rather neglected one.

The theme of the flight into Egypt was a common one in Flemish art of the time, though generally the Holy Family is depicted not on the road but during a rest, as in a pen drawing by Bruegel himself, in Berlin.

Bruegel did two versions of *The Tower of Babel* (Plate 13) besides the miniature done in collaboration with Clovio, which we have already discussed. This version, now in Vienna, is stronger and more dramatic than the one in Rotterdam, which, despite the fact that it is preferred by some scholars, is less evocative. In the Rotterdam version the tower is depicted as being complete up to the eighth floor, while in this version the tower appears almost mangled, thus producing a much more striking effect. In addition, a highly effective chromatic device is created by the contrast between the red of the bricks and the yellowish color of the marble exterior and the rock upon which the huge structure stands.

There is certainly a memory of the Colosseum in this extraordinary representation, and the long aqueduct in the left background recalls the aqueducts in the Roman countryside. Seen from above, this monstrous pagan cathedral (Van Mander rightly observes that ''from above one can see the inside'') is swarming with workmen who are so tiny as to make the tower even more immense. These workers, machines, and building tools, capstans and keystones, indicate a considerable experience and interest in such operations on Bruegel's part, on the basis of which the city of Brussels assigned him the task of depicting the work on the canal linking Brussels to Antwerp.

The huge size of the tower is also enhanced by the fact that in certain parts it appears to be complete and inhabited (flowers, laundry hung out to dry) and by the tiny size of the Gothic city on the left, as well as by the traffic of ships and rafts which are bringing building materials. The entire painting swarms with microscopic life. In the left foreground are the monarch with his small retinue and the stonemasons, some of whom are on their knees before the king while others continue to work.

The Tower of Babel, like Saul, is another Biblical example of the sin of pride, which is mentioned by Dante (*Purgatory* XII, 34):

> I saw Nimrod at the foot of his great structure as if bewildered and looking at the people who, in Shinar, were proud of him.

One wonders if Bruegel was familiar with *The Divine Comedy,* a not unlikely supposition, since the artist was a man of culture, who had been in Italy for three or four years and had frequented Clovio's Roman friends.

With *The Tower of Babel* and *The Way to Calvary,* both from 1564, begins Bruegel's extraordinary but unfortunately brief activity in Brussels—five short years of intense creativity.

With *The Way to Calvary* (Plate 14), which is the largest of his paintings, Bruegel returns to his favorite subject, the anonymous undifferentiated crowd. The theme had already been treated in a similar manner by Aertsen and Jan Van Amstel (the "Monogramist of Brunswick," Coecke's brother-in-law), and can be related to a frequent experience in the tormented life of the times, the executions of the Spanish Inquisition. Van Mander cites this work as being in the collection of Rudolph II, describing it as "very natural, with some comical scenes"; it also appears among the works left by Jongelinck to the city of Antwerp in 1566.

"Comical scenes" abound in this diverting Bruegelian creation: Simon of Cyrene resisting the soldiers while his wife furiously defends him; the cart of robbers assisted by friars. The spectator's eye is constantly attracted by this or that figure, by minor episodes, to the extent that Christ falling beneath the cross does not particularly attract notice, hidden as He is among the red tunics of the soldiers.

But the most extraordinary aspect of this teeming composition is the gust which carries like specks of straw the 500 people in it from left to right, in a curve whose pivot is formed by the incredible craggy rock shaped like a huge decayed tooth, on top of which is a windmill. Even the sky contributes to this motion; from bright on the left it becomes dark on the right, in a way reminiscent of *The Port of Naples.* Even more incredible is the group of women in the foreground (Plate 15), pathetic figures that seem to be taken directly from a *Lamentation over the Dead Christ* or from a *Crucifixion.* This is a surprising echo of the fifteenth century, almost as if Bruegel had wanted to make up in some way for his too lighthearted and profane treatment of a sacred subject. Several figures of mourners to the right of this group add an additional touch of sorrow to these archaic figures. Hauser's interpretation, that in the group of Marys we see a fusion of Gothic and Mannerism, is not very plausible. At any rate, we should note that to the right of this group, in place of the traditional skull of Adam, is that of a large animal, perhaps a horse. This presence is no less magic than that of the thistle bush below it with its explosive vitality. The wheel on the long pole at the far right is a visual repetition of the circle of spectators in the background awaiting the execution.

Among the most convincing local precedents to this work is a painting by the mysterious Monogramist of Brunswick, *The Entry of Christ into Jerusalem* (Stuttgart, Staatsgalerie). This artist's example, writes Philippot, "certainly helped Bruegel to integrate the action into the unity of the landscape. . . . Bruegel, we must say, immediately surpasses his model. . . ."

The Monogramist of Brunswick is identified by some scholars as Jan Van Amstel (Coecke's brother-in-law), or as Jan Van Hemessen; whoever he was, he was an important factor in the development of Bruegel's work.

The Adoration of the Magi (Plate 16) is unique among Bruegel's works, because of its unusual vertical format and because the

breughel . Inuentor .
H·Cock excu. cū priui

P.
ME.

LVXVRIA.

LVXVRIA   ENERVAT   VIRES,   EFFOEMINAT   ARTVS.

Luxurye   stinckt / sy   is   vol   onsuuerheden   Sy   breeckt   die   Craehten / en   sy   swackt   die   leden

Lust
engraving

Biblical event is not lost in an anonymous crowd as in his other works. In fact, this work is conceived in an almost Italian format. All these factors lead one to believe that this picture was commissioned as an altarpiece destined for a side chapel dedicated to the Wise Men and that it was rejected by the church on account of its mocking spirit. Thus Bruegel anticipated by half a century Caravaggio's profane approach to sacred subjects and the reaction that such an approach provoked. Unfortunately, no documentary evidence exists to either support or deny this supposition.

The scene of The Adoration of the Magi is depicted from above, elongating the figures in a Manneristic fashion. The origin of this composition has intrigued critics, who have seen Correggio as the source of the diagonal receding composition, Parmigianino for the elongated figures, Michelangelo's Bruges Madonna for the figure of the Virgin, as well as echoes of Raphael and Sebastiano del Piombo. This list of possible sources seems a trifle excessive, especially since it seems to disregard completely Bruegel's own powerful imagination. The three wise men, Saint Joseph, and the halberdier form a circle around the Virgin; two other men (perhaps portraits) and, behind them, the group of soldiers break the impression of a closed circle. Dvořak has noted a mixture of the grotesque and the mysterious in this painting: opaque stupidity and indifference together with a sense of solemnity, in details such as the man whispering in the corpulent Saint Joseph's ear; the two astonished-looking men behind the black king; and the elongated figures of the kings, particularly the old king with the extremely long sleeve; while the black king, splendidly attired in his fringed yellow robe, offers his magnificent gift, a little golden ship with a seashell, out of which peeps a monkey with a huge pearl.

This strange Adoration of the Magi dates from the same time as another religious work, the grisaille Death of the Virgin (Plate 17), as well as two other Biblical subjects, The Resurrection (Rotterdam, Museum Boymans-Van Beuningen) and Christ and the Adulteress (London, Seilern Collection; there is also a copy in the Accademia Carrara in Bergamo). All of these works are religious subjects, dealt with in a seriously religious fashion. The Death of the Virgin appears in the Rubens inventory of 1640: "The death of Our Lady, in black and white by Bruegel the Elder." The work was painted for Bruegel's friend Abraham Ortelius, who had a print of it made for himself and for his friends ("Sic Petri Brugelij archetypum Philipp. Galleus imitabatur/ Abraham Ortelius sibi et amici fieri curabat/1574").

This painting is a dramatic mixture of mystery and ordinary life, and is Bruegel's only "interior." Its popular tone can be seen as a precursor to Caravaggio, while the many lights which break up the darkness of the interior prefigure Rembrandt — the fire in the hearth, the candle on the round table covered with dishes, the candle in St. Peter's hand, and, above all, the light which emanates from the dying Virgin. These lights create a mystical atmosphere that contrasts with the more plebeian elements such as the sleeping young man near the fireplace, the cat, and the crowd coming in from the doorway, which breaks up the closed impression of the main group, as in The Adoration of the Magi.

From Bruegel's years in Brussels, and precisely from 1565, comes his masterpiece, the series of The Months commissioned by Niclaes Jongelinck, a rich mer-

...wo Blind Men and a Peasant Woman
...erlin, Kupferstichkabinett

chant of Antwerp, to decorate a room in his princely home (two other rooms were decorated by a painter who at the time was more popular than Bruegel, the Romanist Frans Floris). This splendid series, however, presents a curious problem: whether it originally included twelve paintings, one for each month, or only six, one for every two months. (Five are known today.)

On February 21, 1566, Jongelinck had to give part of his collection as security to the city of Antwerp: a Dürer, twenty Floris, and sixteen Bruegels, described as "*The Twelve Months, The Way to Calvary,* and *The Tower of Babel.*" This would lead one to believe that there were twelve paintings of the Months, especially since all twenty of the pictures by Floris are precisely listed in the document. On the other hand, it is difficult to explain how six large pictures by Bruegel could have disappeared without a trace.

On July 3, 1591, the city of Antwerp made a gift to the Archduke Ernest (as documented in a note by Ernest's secretary Hütter) of six paintings: "The lords of Antwerp give to His Highness six paintings representing the twelve Months. . ." This seems to demonstrate that in fact there were only six pictures, each of which covered two months. In 1657 these paintings reappeared in the collection of Archduke Leopold William, who until the preceding year had been governor of the Low Countries, but in his collection only five pictures are listed.

This problem has long been a topic of discussion for scholars, and it still remains unsolved. Grossmann and Jedlika strongly believe that there were originally twelve paintings; De Tolnay and others believe there were only six, two for each month, a representation that was common, though not at that time. Not only has the number of paintings been open to question, but also the identification of the months represented. According to Grossmann, who is quite reliable, the five surviving paintings should be identified as follows: *Hunters in the Snow* is January; *Cloudy Day* is February; *The Hay Harvest* is July; *The Harvesters* is August; and *The Return of the Herd* is November, or perhaps October.

But let us now leave behind this thorny question and consider the reality of these beautiful paintings, in which Bruegel reached the most intense, moving, and poetic point in his art. That year, 1565, must have been a very happy one, in which the painter could depict with complete freedom a subject which responded perfectly to his own genuine interests. What is represented here is no longer the work of the poor, whose humble existence, subject to the mysterious influence of the stars, had been depicted in the calendars of late Gothic books of hours. Instead we witness the solemn, solitary, and blessed work of man on the face of the earth, in harmony with a provident Nature. An intense cosmic feeling pervades these depictions of the days, months, seasons, and toils of the Flemish countryside, which also have a universal significance: man's labor in the eternal cycle of the changing seasons, and the fruits of a fertile and benevolent earth. We no longer see here the anonymous, indifferent crowd, but rather men working side by side, a few laborers working in harmony beneath the clemency of the heavens. Bruegel's virile, optimism had never had such a full expression as in these pictures that form the verses of a serene hymn to the beauty and variety of the world. And, significantly, these paintings do not lend themselves to subtle iconographic interpretations.

The tumultuous stormy day in early spring, the luminosity of the hay harvest, the cold light of the snowy landscape, and the blinding gold of the crops are all depicted with a constant intensity and an almost miraculous expressive felicity, which seems even more remarkable when one considers the short period of time and the unsure political and personal situation in which these works were produced.

Hunters in the Snow (Plate 18) — what month does it represent? For Glück it is February, as in the *Très Riches Heures du Duc De Berry* or the Grimani Breviary (we should recall that Cardinal Grimani was Clovio's patron, and that Bruegel more than likely met him in Rome); other scholars see it as November or December. But all this seems like idle conjecture when one looks at the magnificent group of hunters and dogs among the trees in the foreground (Plate 19), and details such as the refined silhouettes of the trees against the sky; or the arabesques formed by the tails, backs, and legs of the dogs who follow the weary hunters over the somewhat livid white of the snow; or the fire blazing outside the inn; or the crow whose flight seems to precede the hunters' progress to the right of the wide expanse of country buried in the snow, including the craggy mountain and the two frozen ponds on which people trade or amuse themselves. The scene has a feeling of silent suspension, as if the world were waiting for more snow.

Against the reddish brown of the foreground in the *Cloudy Day* (Plate 20) we see a group of bare trees, one man pruning a willow and another tying faggots, and a little boy with a lantern and crown (signifying perhaps the Magi or Carnival) in the dim hour of twilight. To the left is the village below, with its thatched cottages, cart, the sign of an inn, and a man calmly urinating against a wall. In the distance are the stormy greenish water and sky, snowy mountain peaks (a memory of Bruegel's Alpine journey), and the black filigree of the leafless trees against the angry sky.

The Hay Harvest (Plate 21) presents a spectacular array of colors, from brown to green to grey to the blue of the hills below the clement sky. The road, the fields, the trees, and the crags all participate in the solemn peace with which the happy rhythm of the people in the foreground harmonizes perfectly. This picture in fact has a highly musical quality; there is a light, dancelike quality in the figures of the three girls going toward the left, while the white horse and the people carrying baskets full of green beans and cherries move in the opposite direction. This opposition renders the rhythm of the scene more lively. One can almost hear the hammering of the man on the left sharpening his scythe. In the central portion of the composition is a cart being loaded with hay while the horses peacefully eat.

One cannot resist comparing this humble, real cart of hay with Bosch's famous hay cart, assailed by the desperate, screaming crowd of both the humble and the powerful — an image of human greed and folly, in contrast to Bruegel's ingenuous depiction, free of any esoteric meaning or allusion. This comparison serves to illustrate Bruegel's serene, ''healthily optimistic'' nature (as Friedländer writes), ''his enthusiastic spirit that loved life despite its tribulations'' — a spirit that expresses itself in these *Months* with enchanting immediacy.

We repeat that Bruegel's ''Boschian'' paintings should be considered the fruit not so much of a secret affinity with Bosch's spirit but rather of the wishes of collectors mad for the "devilries" of the master of Hertogenbosch, just as the many drawings that Bruegel made for Cock's prints were to satisfy the requests of people who found both delight and horror in Boschian parables, visions, and nightmares. We are too inclined to attribute to the artists of the past the conditions of the modern artist, who rarely works on commission and is generally free to follow his own inspiration; in Bruegel's time, however, there was a patron behind every work, with his own ideas and wishes. At times, as in the case of the *Months,* the patron's desires happily coincided with the artist's preferences, or else the patron gave the artist complete liberty.

There is another cart in *The Harvesters* (Plate 22), on the far side of the golden wall of wheat, which shows up blond against the green of the countryside that stretches out between the wheat fields, groves, and banks of the lake. This view has not without reason been considered as a precise memory of Bruegel's journey to Italy, that is, Geneva and her lake seen from the foot of Mt. Salene. At any rate this is a coherent landscape, not a composite one as in the other paintings of this series, and forms an idyllic backdrop to the blinding light and sense of heat in the foreground scene. This is the highest poetic expression not only in this series but perhaps in all of Bruegel's paintings; in this picture cosmic inspiration and the painter's fraternal affection for human labor are united with perfect felicity.

The tree in the foreground divides the scene into two parts: on the left is depicted the backbreaking work of the busy harvesters, who are a far cry from the heroic and almost Michelangelesque quality of the figures of Bruegel's drawing of *Summer* in Hamburg; on the right is the already mown field, where a woman is tying the wheat into sheaves, a seeming prefiguration of Van Gogh. At the foot of the tree a group of workers are refreshing themselves, seated in the shade on dry sheaves, the women wearing their wide-brimmed "Vietnamese" hats. One harvester is asleep with his legs apart, prefiguring the happy repose of *The Land of Cockaigne.*

The Return of the Herd (Plate 23) is in a poor state of conservation, so that the colors are bland and the bodies of the animals appear flat. This is a traditional landscape, seen from above, with a diagonal river and a menacing sky on the left, which creates a contrasting movement to that of the herd, intensifying the sense of toil and effort. The reddish, burnt colors indicate autumn, as do the harvested vineyard and the net for catching migrating birds.

With regard to the short period of time in which Bruegel executed this cycle of paintings, Grossmann writes that "it is possible only for an artist who is completely master of his technique, which here reveals a spontaneity, a rapid and almost compendiary method, which is very different from the elaborate execution of Bruegel's preceding works. At times the preparation of the canvas shows through in order to attain certain coloristic effects; the paint is applied very lightly, with an almost dry brush, a technique taken up and advanced by Rubens."

In the same year that he painted the *Months* Bruegel found time to paint the *Winter Landscape with Bird Snare* (Plate 24), executed with extreme finesse in the misty yellowish atmosphere beneath the opaque winter sky, which is very different from the crisp, crystalline air of *Hunters in the Snow.* Critics are almost unanimous in considering this painting in the Delporte

Summer
Hamburg, Hamburger Kunsthalle

Colllection as the autograph Bruegel that was reproduced and copied numerous times, and should be considered as an archetype of the innumerable winter landscapes in seventeenth-century Flemish painting.

In this vast, silent landscape, with its bare trees and houses covered with snow, the only movement is that of the skaters on the frozen canal and the restless fluttering of the birds around the snare. The critics who try to discover in Bruegel's every brush stroke a meaning or moral have interpreted this painting as representing two imminent dangers: the ice for the skaters and the snare for the birds.

There are two versions of *The Massacre of the Innocents* (Plate 25): one in Vienna, which is reproduced here, and the other in Hampton Court. According to Grossmann's reliable judgment, the version in Vienna is a workshop copy, with some autograph portions by Bruegel; the Hampton court picture is the original, and despite its poor state of conservation, with repaintings and alterations (instead of the baby in the foreground scene, there is a calf!), Grossmann considers it to be far superior in its intact portions. This retouched version was taken from the imperial collection in Prague in the Swedish sack of 1648, passed to Queen Christina of Sweden's collection, and then to Hampton Court.

This painting was described by Van Mander when it was in the possession of Rudolph II: "A massacre of the innocents, in which various realistic scenes are depicted, . . . including a scene where a family of peasants pleads for the life of a baby whom a cruel soldier has taken to put to death. The mourning and desolation of the mothers, as well as other equally moving episodes, are rendered in a remarkable way."

The painting is not dated. Many scholars have attempted to relate it to the cruel deeds of the Duke of Alba in 1567. But two copies (in Antwerp and Brussels) by Pieter Bruegel the Younger bear the date 1564.

The originality of this scene is strongly emphasized by the snowy background on which it takes place. There are violent clashes of people and horses, scenes of desperation and inhuman cruelty, and doors being broken down. The group of armed soldiers on horseback forms a wall of iron enclosing the agonizing, convulsive scene.

Bruegel again took up the format of a populous scene in a snowy setting against which the small figures stand out like colored insects in *The Census at Bethlehem* (Plate 26), which could be considered as a companion piece to *The Massacre of the Innocents*. The subject here is another Biblical story, that of Joseph and Mary going to Bethlehem for the census (Luke II:1–5), but this is a Flemish Bethlehem, with the diversions and labors of a village of Bruegel's time, and with everyone attending to his own affairs: a man slits a pig's throat and a woman catches the blood in a long-handled frying pan; chickens feed next to the cart; people crowd around the "Inn of the Green Crown" (which bears the emblem of Charles V) to declare their names and pay the tithe. On the frozen ponds people amuse themselves with sleds, skates, and tops; some transport goods; toward the background carpenters are putting up the frame of a house; people are grouped outside the "Inn of the Swan" and a hollowed-out tree; a man urinates against a wall, while behind the stiff branches of the tall tree the sun is setting, depicted as a red ball, which suggests a possible Japanese influence. Life goes on as usual and no one

Spring
Vienna, Albertina

notices Mary on the ass with Saint Joseph, who carries on his shoulder a huge saw and at his waist an auger to declare his trade as a carpenter.

In this minute swarm of small figures, against the backdrop of houses, towers, and bastions, the restless yet alert eye of the painter amuses itself, indulging what could be termed his "anarchistic" tendencies. There is no hierarchy here: everyone participates yet no one dominates the scene; there is no protagonist — what counts is the community, the choral feeling, the tranquil flow of everyday life, contemplated with an eye full of sympathy and poetry and of love for the common people.

We can imagine Bruegel's friend Ortelius coming to visit him in Brussels and the discussion they might have had about this picture: "My dear Pieter, you know perfectly well that it never snowed in Bethlehem; that is a warm country. . . ." "Certainly, but I like to picture the scene as if it were happening not in remote times but here and now; and people show up better against the snow. . . ." "But how in the world can those people not know that the man with the woman on the ass are sacred characters? No one notices them; no one gives any sign of seeing them!" "How would they know that it's Saint Joseph with Mary, who is about to give birth? Those are things that people found out later, much later, certainly not in that moment. My dear Abraham, when you were born (or when our beloved Erasmus was born) no one went around saying: 'A great scientist, a marvelous philosopher has been born.' No, it took years and years of toil and nights spent by candlelight for the world to realize it." "All right, but the Italians do things differently, they depict the event in the foreground, separate from the rest of the picture."

"That's true; I tried that myself, in my painting of The Epiphany, but it doesn't suit me. I like to imagine things as they really happened. In the picture of Christ carrying the cross, do you think that people realized who that man falling on the ground was, and that a horrible crime was being committed, the crime of nailing God to a cross? Of course not, people were enjoying themselves; they came to see the spectacle; things went on as always. That's how we northern artists paint: not just me, look at Pieter Aertsen or Jan Van Amstel and many others. We see the truth of nature, and the mystery of life, and the beauty of nature. Look in the corner where I painted that beautiful thistle and that horse's skull. . . ."

Shortly afterward Bruegel returned to a subject he had already dealt with a couple of times (in a very faded tempera from around 1556 in Brussels, and in the painting in London), The Adoration of the Magi in the Snow (Plate 27), and to the pleasure of immersing a sacred scene in a depiction of everyday life, with people not only on the snow, but in the snow, under a heavy snowstorm. This painting appeared in the inventory of the French banker Eberhard Jubach in 1696: "Winter, with many small figures; in the foreground the three kings who adore Our Lord; the snow falls heavily, a little boy plays with his sled on the ice: by Bruegel the Elder."

And really more than to the sacred event, which is confined to a corner in the left foreground, one's eye is drawn to the activities of the many figures who populate the scene: two men who have broken the ice to draw water, or the little boy playing with his sled, pushing himself with two poles with sharpened iron points. These children's sleds (there are two in The Census at Bethlehem) were fashioned from a

44

cow's or horse's jawbones, and are yet another indication of Bruegel's attention to even the smallest details.

Cleaning (1942) has freed the *Wedding Dance in the Open Air* (Plate 28) from the repainting that had sullied it, revealing an authentic masterpiece, despite the thinness of its colors. Denis affirms: "The color is so diaphanous that the preparatory drawing of the figures clearly shows through, with which the artist intended to suggest the movement of the dance."

The scene is depicted from above, with only a glimpse of the horizon, in lively colors that enhance the vertiginous movement, the frenzied, almost animalesque violence, and at the same time stupendously effective rhythm of the dancers: the swishing of the women's skirts, the savage aggressivity and satyrlike expression of the men, with their swollen trouser-flaps — one of Bruegel's few explicitly sexual references. The dance and the bagpipes have been interpreted as symbolic of lust; in Rabelais, as well, this rustic musical instrument has a sexual meaning.

The eight couples of dancers are arranged in a triangle whose apex is the tree. The many onlookers are immobile, but the movement of the dance is so intense that it animates the entire composition. In the background is a draped table and a curtain with the crown of the bride, who is probably the woman dancing without a bonnet, her reddish hair hanging free. Of the many replicas of this composition (in Narbonne, Antwerp, and Philadelphia), De Tolnay claims to have found the original in a miniature on vellum (183 × 218 mm) in the Uffizi in Florence (*Gazzette des Beaux Arts,* 1969), but this leaves us rather perplexed, since this extremely free, lively picture in Detroit has the vigor of an original creation.

In *The Preaching of St. John the Baptist,* the presence of contemporary life is very evident. Bruegel had certainly witnessed and been impressed by the spectacle of frequent clandestine Protestant sermons ("hagepreken"), which drew large crowds from among the common people. Behind the colored barrier of the people's backs in the foreground are the tiny figures of the people listening to John the Baptist, who is pointing at Christ. Their faces are astonished and their eyes wide open, as in a painting by Pontormo; the strange multicolored costumes of soldiers, friars, and gypsies stand out in the foreground. A curious detail is the man with his back to St. John having his palm read by a gypsy with a colorful mantle, which is an open note of dissent: such sermons were condemned by Calvin and prohibited by law in Flanders. This man has been interpreted by some critics to be a portrait of Bruegel's friend Franckert, and the bearded soldier with his hand over his mouth has been seen as a self-portrait, though with little or no supporting evidence.

The Conversion of St. Paul (Plate 29), as recounted in *The Acts of the Apostles* (IX:3), was cited by Van Mander as being in the collection of Emperor Rudolph II ("with well-made mountains"). We know that in 1567 the Duke of Alba crossed the Alps to quell the Flemish revolutionaries, and some critics see this picture as an allusion to those events. At any rate, Bruegel's attention here is concentrated on the magnificent Alpine landscape, with its red and yellow rocks and crags, its strangely groomed pine trees, and the picturesque, brightly colored costumes of the soldiers who are advancing from the deep ravine on the left toward the background on the right. The Biblical episode is no more than a minimal incident, with Saul struck by lightning on this rocky and improbable road to Damascus. The largest figures are the cavalrymen and foot soldiers seen from the back in the right foreground, in a luxurious display of costumes and colors. This picture can be related to *The Suicide of Saul,* for its scenic format as well as for the minimization of the Biblical story, which is little more than a pretext for the representation.

One of Bruegel's most famous works is the *Peasant Wedding Feast* (Plate 30), which takes place in a granary or barn. This work is unique both because of its enclosed scene and because of the fact that it depicts people eating, which is rare in Bruegel's works (another example is in *The Harvesters*).

The perspective format of this scene has suggested a derivation from Tintoretto's *Wedding Feast at Cana* (1561), which Bruegel might have known about from his traveling companion Marten de Vos, who had worked with Tintoretto for a decade in Venice. One critic has even gone so far as to suggest that it was this painting by Bruegel that inspired Tintoretto's *Last Supper* in San Giorgio Maggiore. A much more plausible hypothesis is that Bruegel's *Wedding Feast* was influenced by a composition by the Monogramist of Brunswick, *The Parable of the Wedding Feast,* as Baccheschi has pointed out.

This picture provides evidence for Van Mander's observation that Bruegel and his friend Franckert "often went to the country and mingled with the peasants on the occasion of an outdoor feast or wedding. Dressed as peasants and declaring themselves to be relatives of the bride or groom, they offered the traditional wedding gift along with the others. Bruegel loved to observe the peasants' way of eating, drinking, dancing, lovemaking, and amusing themselves. He knew how to reproduce these things in a pleasing, lively way, in tempera or oil — these two techniques held no secrets for him. He was a master at depicting these peasants of the Campine (a region to the east of Antwerp) in their clothing and ornaments; with great naturalness he showed their clumsy dancing, their way of walking, and other facts and gestures of everyday life."

The colorful, relatively tranquil company is seated around a rustic table painted in perspective (Jedlika has observed that the chair jutting out on the right gives the diagonal and vertical lines of the composition). The guests sitting around the giddy bride, in front of a green curtain, with a crown on her head are not too numerous (an edict from Charles V limited them to twenty). It is difficult to tell who the groom is — traditionally he served the guests — perhaps he is the man in black on the left who is filling the pitchers (which constitute a noteworthy still life in themselves). In a corner on the right a monk is conversing with a man with a reddish beard, traditionally considered to be a self-portrait. This scene is depicted with a lively variety of characters, attitudes, poses, and colors, against the luminous backdrop of the hay. The people coming in at the door break up the closed impression of the main scene.

One thing has not been observed that is worthy of note in Bruegel's work: the fact that despite his predilection for the rustic life and peasant customs Bruegel never presents a true "interior." The celebrations and dances he depicts are almost always in the open air, without spatial (or moral) restrictions. What interests him is collective merrymaking, the overwhelming rhythm of the dance, or, as in this scene, the meal of the

Landscape with a Rabbit Hunter
etching

wedding celebration. We never find in his works the depiction of the interior of a house, the domestic hearth, the intimacy of a peasant family; just as he rarely depicts people in repose — he has a constant passion for movement, whether it be work or play, a constant passion for space, for the open air, for light and motion. Understandably, therefore, his masterpiece is the series of *Months,* which are a felicitous meeting of his creative powers and his favorite subject. Grossmann sees the *Wedding Feast* as a representation of gluttony (and of lust and anger in its companion piece, the *Peasant Wedding Dance*). But really one does not have the impression of excessive voracity or revelry; the food in the plates carried by the two men on a rough plank of wood doesn't appear to be too bountiful. The theme of gluttony is often present in Bruegel's work: from *The Battle between Carnival and Lent* to *The Land of Cockaigne* we find encounters between the fat and the lean, the well-fed and the famished. In one picture from around 1559 (Statens Museum for Kunst, Copenhagen) appears a *Fat Head* (perhaps a cleric) assailed by a thin couple, the male member of which is even biting the fat man's cheek. There are two engravings after drawings by Bruegel, *The Fat Kitchen* and *The Thin Kitchen* (1563), with eloquent representations: in the first the fat, greasy diners are throwing out a skeletal man who wants to take part in their feast, while the second print shows a group of painfully thin men throwing a fat man out of the door.

The depiction of people actually in the act of eating, however, is rare in Bruegel's work — we see it only in *The Harvesters* and here in the *Peasant Wedding Feast,* while the sated characters of *The Land of Cockaigne* are seen immersed in the ec-static process of digestion. At any rate, allusions to a full stomach or even more frequently an empty one are often, and eloquently, present in Bruegel's work: the spoon which at times appears in men's hatbands instead of a feather or a flower is a clear declaration of a constant willingness to use one's jaws.

The picture which is probably the companion piece to the *Wedding Feast* is the *Peasant Wedding Dance* (Plate 32). This work, as well, is seen from a slightly higher angle than normally, and the figures in the foreground — the couple dancing with savage energy and the enormous bagpipe player with the porcine face who is being admired by the boy bringing him something to drink — are of an unusual monumentality. Beside the bagpipe player are the tiny figures of a girl teaching a baby to dance, which have a compositional function similar to that of the little girl greedily licking a plate in the *Wedding Feast* (Plate 31). Around the table are peasants drinking and shouting, a couple clumsily kissing, and other couples dancing in front of the tavern with the red banner. In the background is a church and in the tree at right is a tiny image of the Madonna, but no one is nursing religious thoughts in this atmosphere of a country celebration.

This picture however does not convey the frenetic rhythm of the *Wedding Dance in the Open Air* in Detroit, which is truly a hymn to unbridled lust.

The Land of Cockaigne or *Luilekkerland* (Plate 33) is an earthly paradise for gluttons and idlers taken from a Flemish legend, according to which Cockaigne was a distant country, to get to which one had to dig a tunnel through a mountain of polenta. On the upper right, in fact, a new guest is emerging from the mountain to join the

The Beekeepers
Berlin, Kupferstichkabinett

three men resting stretched out on the small meadow, in a crystalline air of peaceful burping, immersed in the long dreamed-of process of digestion.

Everything is edible in this land: the hedges tied with sausages and the appetizing food on the circular table. If that weren't enough, a roast pig runs about offering itself to be eaten, with a knife stuck into its crisp skin, like the soft-boiled egg and the chicken on the platter. On the right is a sort of cactus made of flat-bread cakes like the ones on the roof of the hut (which we have already seen in *Flemish Proverbs*), under which is an armed soldier with his mouth wide open and a roast pigeon flying in (this detail is difficult to see because of a careless cleaning of the painting); nearby is a red-crusted cheese, and the very little background left by the high point of view is taken up by a lake which seems to be of broth, as in Teofilo Folengo: "Illic ad bassum currunt flumina brodae/quae lagum suppae generant..."

Such is the country where the three men blissfully doze, arranged like the spokes of a wheel around the foot of the tree: the soldier (depicted in a bold foreshortening, which some critics have seen as a reflection of Tintoretto's *Miracle of the Slave*), beside whom is lying his useless lance; the fat, greasy peasant, sleeping on a thresher's flail; and finally the scholar, stretched out on the soft fur that lines his cloak and dreaming with his eyes (alive like grains of pepper) wide open. This is an enchanting image, to which the painter has applied himself with acute attention, as we can easily see by observing the two figures in the foreground and the contrast they form — not only the richness and color of the scholar's clothing contrasted to the simplicity of the shirt and brown pants of the peasant, which clearly reveal his round shape, but also the "centrifugal" position of the scholar with his legs spread wide apart and his hands under his head, while the peasant represents the perfect formal inversion of this figure, as he is completely closed within himself, "centripetal." The whole is painted with obvious relish and variation, as seen in the infinite variety of shades of green in the terrain.

This hymn to the pleasures of the table is dated 1567, the same year that the Duke of Alba unchained his cruel repression. One of the many critics who like to speculate on the hidden meanings of Bruegel's paintings, Francis sees this picture as a warning, as if the painter were saying to the powerful: "Look how our country would be without your inhumanities and cruelties and condemnations."

There are two temperas by Bruegel which somehow made their way to Parma and from there to Naples: *The Blind Leading the Blind* and *The Misanthrope* (Plates 34–36). The tragic sequence of the blind men being dragged to their death, according to the evangelical parable (Matthew XV:14 and Luke VI:39), is, along with *The Triumph of Death* and perhaps more than that picture, the most desperate invention created by Bruegel, despite his serene character. But the theme of the blind men often returns in Bruegel's works — in *The Battle between Carnival and Lent* and in a drawing (Berlin) of *Two Blind Men and a Peasant Woman* — and in fact they were a common sight in the squares and streets of Flanders. Dvořak sees a relation between the landscape in this picture and Venetian painting; other critics instead have tried to identify it with geographic precision: Pede Sainte Anne, near Brussels, past Dilbeck, to the left of the road to Ninova.

This is a terrifying, unforgettable painting, with its subdued colors (the medium is tempera, absorbed by the canvas, whose grain can be easily seen), the six blind men perceived with an extraordinarily penetrating eye and depicted with confidence, their cloaks flying, leaning against one another, with a cane in their hands or a hand on their companion's shoulder. The blind men are shown with a variety of expressions, that sense of questioning desperation that one sees in blind sockets. In the background is a luminous landscape, including a church, a tree, and a cottage. A tremendous descending rhythm carries the blind men toward their inevitable end (Plate 35) — a true image of humanity, both the blind and those who can see — a terrible image of fatality. Grossmann writes: "Just as we see old age through the eyes of Rembrandt, so we are in Bruegel's debt for the image of blindness." Certainly Baudelaire was thinking of this picture in his poem *The Blind Men:* "Contemplate them, my soul; they are truly frightening / They seem like mannequins; vaguely ridiculous; / Terrifying. . ."

In this as in other works, the precision with which the painter depicts various infirmities has led a French medical student (Torrilhon) to write a thesis on the representation of illnesses in Bruegel, who Torrilhon believes had a knowledge of medicine.

Its companion piece, *The Misanthrope* (Plate 36), has provoked some doubts about its inscription, its date, and also the man in the crystal globe (a symbol of the world, as seen in the *Flemish Proverbs*), which according to one critic is a later addition.

The inscription says, "Since the world is so evil, I dress in mourning," supposedly the words of the old man wrapped in a black cloak and hood, so that all we can see are his nose, his white beard, and his hands — the imperious protagonist of the painting. Friedländer, talking about Bruegel's shift from pictures swarming with minute figures to paintings dominated by a single character, says: "Bruegel is no longer firing bullets, but cannonballs." We should also note that, from the traditional grandiose composite landscapes of his earlier pictures, toward the end of his life Bruegel turned to depicting the flat Flemish countryside, here with a windmill and a shepherd with his flock.

This tondo is generally taken to be an expression of profound pessimism on the part of Bruegel, a painter disillusioned by the world, which could be true. But it is also possible that a cynical man of letters asked Bruegel to depict this subject: "Make me a painting of an old man in a black cloak, and on the road put thorns with four spines and on the meadow poisonous mushrooms, to signify human perfidy. . . ." That the painter gave his own personal touch to this idea is certain, as we can see from the beauty of the picture.

The Cripples (Plate 37), with its highly refined color, presents a ghastly group of five unfortunates supported by crutches, afflicted with incredible physical deformities, which create a sad effect on our sensibilities. But this was not an uncommon sight on the streets of Flanders in Bruegel's time: sickness, misery, mendacity were continually before everyone's eyes; there were no asylums and hospitals like the ones that nowadays spare us from such sights. Dvořak compares these unhappy creatures to "a family of poisonous mushrooms germinated from the damp ground of a solitary corner." A similar group appears in *The Battle between Carnival and Lent,* and one of those beggars too wears a fox's tail on his little cape. The significance of these tails has been the subject of much discussion: according to some they are the mark of lepers; to others, of beggars or *gueux*, a name later assumed by the rebels of the "Compromise," whom an official of Margaret of Parma had disdainfully called by that name, but this explanation is rather perplexing.

On the back of the panel are two Latin distics (dictated perhaps by Ortelius) that say: "Not even Nature possesses what our art lacks, so great is a painter's privilege; here Nature, translated into painted images and seen in her cripples, is astounded to realize that Bruegel is equal to her." This is a typically humanistic eulogy; the first line is taken from the epitaph Politian wrote for Giotto.

Another important observation that should be made regarding this painting is how the green of the bushes between the red brick walls vibrates with tiny points of light, a new technique which Bruegel used in his latest works and which will triumph in *The Magpie on the Gallows* and *The Robber of Birds' Nests*.

In *The Robber of Birds' Nests* (Plate 38) we find another proverb or Flemish folk saying: "He who knows where the nest is, knows it; he who takes it, owns it." The corpulent peasant is pictured frontally (he has been seen as a derivation from a figure in Michelangelo's *The Conversion of St. Paul*!), his unexpressive face plastically modeled by the brush strokes, his eyes round and wide open, as in Pontormo. One critic has seen the iris in the left foreground of this picture as a symbol of man fortified against temptation (but an iris also appears near the pit into which the poor blind men in the preceding painting fall!), the brambles as victory over temptation, and the twisted willow stump as a symbol of thievery.

But what is important to observe in this painting is its luminosity, the subtlety of the reflections on the trunks of the birches, the grass, the landscape stretching out beneath the expanse of sky. In fact, Bruegel here has abandoned the composite landscape made up of recollections and combinations that he had used, from the time of the *Landscape with Sower* on, to depict the flat countryside of the Campine, that is, the reality of his everyday life. He has also abandoned the swarming, anonymous crowds of small figures of his earlier works in order to limit himself to a single protagonist, as he had already done in *The Misanthrope*, or to a few figures in the foreground. This new monumentality is seen by Philippot as a result of the influence of Michelangelo's Pauline Chapel frescoes; by enlarging his figures Bruegel "carried out, in the course of 1568, the last year of his life, one of the most unprecedented and striking renewals a painter has ever had at the end of his career."

It is no exaggeration to say that *The Magpie on the Gallows* (Plate 39) is Bruegel's most joyful painting; it is pervaded by a bucolic happiness, a rejoicing lyricism (which has been called "paradisiacal") in the luminosity of the vast landscape seen from above. Bruegel's brush strokes here, as in *The Robber of Birds' Nests*, have a *spiccato* quality which seems to anticipate Vermeer's miraculous points of light. From the woods emerge the peasants in their brightly colored costumes, dancing to the music of the bagpipe; they approach the gallows, on which sits a black and white magpie, with another on the ground at its foot, together with that mysterious horse's skull which had already appeared in *The*

Two Citydwellers Seen from the Rear
Brussels, Bibliothèque royale Albert Ier

Way to Calvary. Bruegel's new pictorial language reaches enchanting heights of lyrical emotion in this painting.

And yet this picture bears the date of 1567, the year of the "bloodbath" of Spanish repression, a fact which makes evident the meaning of the work, as expressed in two Flemish sayings: "To dance beneath the gallows," and another which describes what the crouching man on the lower left is doing. Thus Bruegel — that sharp man, timid and bold at the same time — was saying that the Flemish people, despite the stakes and gallows and the atrocities of the Duke of Alba, were still able to dance and make merry and digest and live their lives.

Van Mander recounts that the dying Bruegel left this painting to his wife, "signifying by the magpie that evil tongues deserved the gallows." And he adds: "There are many prints of the master's curious compositions. He had also done many others in a very careful manner, with inscriptions, but finding them too caustic, he had his wife destroy them during his last illness, fearing they might cause her trouble."

The *Storm at Sea* (Plate 40), which is considered Bruegel's last work, therefore dating from 1569, is perhaps the picture listed in Pieter Stevens' collection in 1668: "Jonas' ship was tossed on the sea, except that here we see no indication of the fearful prophet, but rather a keg floating between the ship and the jaws of the sea monster. This last creation, as well, illustrates a folk proverb: "If you follow the barrel, you lose the boat." An eighteenth-century text reads: "If the whale plays with the keg that has been thrown to him, and thus gives the ship time to escape, this represents the man who loses the true good for an illusion." And some critics have interpreted the church in the distance on the left as the element of salvation that preserves man from the perils of life as represented by the storm.

But all these allusions are forgotten when one looks at this truly apocalyptic vision of the ocean stirred up by a terrible force, whose cosmic feeling brings to mind *Moby Dick*. Bruegel here, in a new style which leaves one dumbfounded, depicts an agitated brown surface with a greenish central portion, under a purplish sky; the strange impression this picture creates is intensified by the fact that it is probably unfinished. At any rate, this is a document of an almost incredible stylistic development. If, in fact, we compare this work to *The Port of Naples* of less than ten years before, it is easy to understand why critics have hesitated to attribute it to Bruegel (in fact, it was originally attributed to Joos de Monper).

Having concluded our close study of the surviving paintings of Pieter Bruegel the Elder, we would like to arrive at a definition of his world, an all-encompassing formula. But one comes to realize that Bruegel's work, while coherent in certain aspects (style and vocabulary, though with rapid developments in the course of only ten years), is extremely varied in others (subjects, meanings). And we must once again stress the influence that his circle of friends and patrons must have had on Bruegel, thus justifying such variety.

Bruegel was a very great artist, with a fascinating cultural formation, but, behind the approximately forty works that can be attributed to him with certainty, he remains a fleeting, hermetic, elusive figure, who operated between the opposite poles of the Erasmian humanists of Antwerp and the peasants of the Flemish countryside. He was a truly unique artist, in the fullest sense

Peasant with Basket
Vienna, Albertina

of the word. In fact, if one thinks of Van Eyck before him and Rubens after him, both of whom dominated the painting of their times, one comes to realize what a singular, solitary artist Bruegel was: with a few slim links to local tradition, and a very few insignificant followers — an artist isloated in the mysterious solitude of genius.

Color Plates

1 - LANDSCAPE WITH SOWER

Oil on panel, 74 × 102 cm
San Diego, Timken Art Gallery

Dated [1]557 and signed [BR]VEGHEL. From the
Stuyck del Bruyère Collection in Antwerp this work
passed to the National Gallery in Washington, and
from there to San Diego. The real subject of this
painting is the landscape with the river, seen
"cartographically" from above and painted according
to the traditional format of a brown foreground, green
central portion, and blue background.

2 - THE PORT OF NAPLES

Oil on panel, 41 × 70 cm
Rome, Doria Pamphili Gallery

This work is unsigned and undated. It appears perhaps
in the Granvelle and Rubens inventories, and in the
Doria Pamphili Gallery in 1794, though its provenance
is unknown. The attribution was proposed by Burchard
in 1912 and is generally accepted, though the date is
still open to discussion.

3 - THE FALL OF ICARUS

Tempera and oil on canvas, 73.5 × 112 cm
Brussels, Musées royaux des Beaux-Arts

There is another, smaller version of this famous picture in the Van Buuren Collection in New York (on panel, 63 × 90 cm), which has important variations: for example, it depicts Dedalus flying and the sun high in the sky, while here it is sunset. Critics are not in agreement as to which is the original.

4 - FLEMISH PROVERBS

Oil on panel, 117 × 163 cm
Berlin, Staatliche Museen Preussischer
Kulturbesitz Gemïaldegalerie
(photo Anders)

Signed and dated, BRUEGEL 1559. This picture depicts about 120 Flemish proverbs or sayings and is also known as a representation of "the world upside down"; it is sometimes called *De Blauwe Huick* (The Blue Cape), because of the depiction at the center of this swarming composition of a wife in red placing a blue cape, the sign of a cuckold, on her old husband's shoulders. It appeared in the Stevens Collection in 1668.

5 - THE BATTLE BETWEEN CARNIVAL AND LENT

Oil on panel, 116 × 164.5 cm
Vienna, Kunsthistorisches Museum
(photo Meyer)

Signed and dated, BRUEGEL 1559. This picture represents the encounter between the Carnival revelers and the Lenten penitents behind and around their two "leaders": the fat Carnival astride a barrel and the famished Lent on a cart pulled by a monk and a nun. The architectural background which frames the scene consists of a church on the right and taverns on the left; the square is a teeming mass of small animated figures.

6 - CHILDREN'S GAMES

Oil on panel, 118 × 161 cm
Vienna, Kunsthistorisches Museum
(photo Meyer)

Signed and dated, BRUEGEL 1560. In the vast square, seen from above as are the two preceding scenes, are numerous colorful and rather clumsy little children, intent on 84 different games. Bruegel had dealt with this theme in preceding miniatures. This picture was acquired by the Archduke Ernest in 1594 and has always remained in the rich Hapsburg collections.

7 - THE TRIUMPH OF DEATH

Oil on panel, 117 × 162 cm
Madrid, Prado

Unsigned and undated, this work dates from around
1562 to 1563. The scene depicts the terrifying vision of
an obscenely triumphant Death and unites the
Medieval theme of the macabre dance with that of the
Last Judgment in a barren landscape seen from above
and swarming with collective scenes or single episodes
up to the horizon, which is obscured by smoke and
flames. It is documented in Antwerp in 1614, and in
1774 was in the Palace of San Ildefonso, from where it
passed in 1827 to the Prado.

8 - THE EXPULSION OF THE REBELLIOUS ANGELS

Oil on panel, 117 × 162 cm
Brussels, Musées royaux des Beaux-Arts

Signed and dated, M.D. LXII BRUEGEL. This work was
acquired by the museum in 1846 as a work by Bruegel
the Younger; it was later attributed to Bosch, until
Bruegel's signature, which had been hidden by the
frame, was discovered. This work has Boschian,
fifteenth-century flavor.

9 - "DULLE GRIET" ("Mad Meg")

Oil on panel, 115 × 161 cm
Antwerp, Mayer Van den Bergh Museum

Signature and date illegible, perhaps 1562. This picture
is a teeming depiction of Boschian elements of
uncertain interpretation. The protagonist advances with
a drawn sword toward the mouth of Hell. The painting
was stolen by the Swedes in the sack of Prague in 1648
and reappeared in the nineteenth century. It was
acquired by the museum in 1894 for 390 marks at an
auction in Cologne.

10 - TWO MONKEYS

Oil on panel, 20 × 23 cm
Berlin, Staatliche Museen Preussischer
Kulturbesitz Gemïaldegalerie
(photo Anders)

Signed and dated, BRUEGEL MDLXII. This work
appeared in the Stevens collection in 1668 as "The city
of Antwerp with two monkeys." It was acquired in
Paris by the Berlin museum in 1930. Various
interpretations of this work have been proposed:
Flanders under Spanish oppression, or man as a slave
to sin. It is much more likely that the painter saw these
two animals and painted them with acute and
penetrating attention, against the background of the city
of Antwerp.

BRVEGEL·MDLXII·

11 - OLD WOMAN

Oil on panel, 22 × 18 cm
Munich, Alte Pinakothek
(photo Blauel)

Unsigned and undated, this work was acquired by the museum in 1912. The attribution to Bruegel has not been accepted by all critics nor is its dating unanimously agreed upon. This seems to be a study from life, and is unique among Bruegel's works.

12 - THE SUICIDE OF SAUL

Oil on panel, 33.5 × 55 cm
Vienna, Kunsthistorisches Museum
(photo Meyer)

Signed and dated BRUEGEL M.CCCCC.LXII, this work also bears the inscription "Saul XXXI CAPIT." The Biblical episode is from Kings 1:31. The soldiers swarming like insects in this complicated rocky landscape, which is depicted with miniaturistic minuteness, recall Bruegel's contact with Mayken Coecke, who was, in fact, a painter of miniatures.

13 - THE TOWER OF BABEL

Oil on panel, 114 × 155 cm
Vienna, Kunsthistorisches Museum
(photo Meyer)

Signed and dated, BRUEGEL.FE.M.CCCCC.LXIII. In 1565 this work appeared in the collection of Niclaes Jongelinck; Van Mander mentions it as being among the works owned by Rudolph II. In 1659 it passed to the gallery of Archduke Leopold William. There is another version of this subject (in a smaller panel, 60 × 74.5 cm, unsigned and undated) in the Boymans-van Beuningen Museum in Rotterdam. It is variously interpreted as a symbol of human folly or as a sign of man's daring and progress.

14 - THE WAY TO CALVARY

Oil on panel, 124 × 170 cm
Vienna, Kunsthistorisches Museum
(photo Meyer)

Signed and dated, BRUEGEL M.D.LXIIII, this is
Bruegel's largest picture. It appeared among the works
possessed by Jongelinck in 1565. This vast landscape
has over 500 characters in it, moving toward the high
ground on the right, where the crosses are surrounded
by a circle of the curious. Like so many other works
now in Vienna, this picture was taken to Paris by the
French (1809–1815) and later returned.

15 - THE WAY TO CALVARY (detail)

Vienna, Kunsthistorisches Museum

16 - THE ADORATION OF THE MAGI

Oil on panel, 108 × 83 cm
London, National Gallery

Signed and dated, BRUEGEL MDLXIIII. This is a unique
work both for its vertical format (which leads one to
believe that it was destined for a church or chapel) and
for the fact that the sacred scene is isolated in the
foreground in an almost Italian fashion. It passed from a
private collection in Vienna to the National Gallery in
1921 and had been in the inventory of the Archduke
Ernest in 1594.

17 - THE DEATH OF THE VIRGIN

Tempera on canvas, 36 × 54.5 cm
London, National Trust
(photo Bethell)

Signed BRUEGEL, with an illegible date (but ca. 1565).
The attribution to Bruegel has been rejected by some
scholars. This work was painted for Bruegel's friend
Abraham Ortelius, who later had a print made of it "for
himself and his friends." It is perhaps one of the works
listed in the possession of Rubens. There are two other
works of a strictly religious character like this grisaille:
The Resurrection (Rotterdam) and *Christ and the
Adulteress* (London). This is one of the extremely rare
interiors in Bruegel's work.

18 - HUNTERS IN THE SNOW

Oil on panel, 117 × 162 cm
Vienna, Kunsthistorisches Museum
(photo Meyer)

Signed and dated, BRUEGEL M.D.LXV. This is one of
the five surviving pieces of the marvelous and
much-discussed series of ''Months''; it is not sure
whether there were twelve, one for each month, or six,
one for every two months. This picture is in an
excellent state of conservation.

19 - HUNTERS IN THE SNOW (detail)

Vienna, Kunsthistorisches Museum

20 - CLOUDY DAY

Oil on panel, 118 × 163 cm
Vienna, Kunsthistorisches Museum
(photo Meyer)

Signed and dated, BRUEGEL MDLXV. Scholars variously interpret this picture as representing the months between January and March; at any rate it clearly alludes to springtime, as is evidenced by the torpid atmosphere and the man pruning. The boy with the lantern and the crown could represent either Epiphany or Carnival.

21 - THE HAY HARVEST

Oil on panel, 114 × 158 cm
Prague, Narodni Galerie

Unsigned and undated, but probably from 1565. From
the Esterhazy collection, this work passed to Prince
Lobkowitz of Raudnitz, and from there to the National
Gallery in Prague. Particularly noteworthy is the
divergent rhythm which animates the figures of the
workers.

22 - THE HARVESTERS

Oil on panel, 118 × 163 cm
New York, Metropolitan Museum of Art

Signed and dated, BRUEGEL [MD]LXV. This work was taken by the French in 1809, along with many other Viennese works that were returned in 1815; but this panel was held back by Count Andreossy, who had a collection of drawings by Bruegel. Its whereabouts were unknown until 1910; in 1912 it was acquired by the Metropolitan. The central scene, with the workers having their meal, is one of the rare examples of people eating in Bruegel's work.

23 - THE RETURN OF THE HERD

Oil on panel, 117 × 159 cm
Vienna, Kunsthistorisches Museum
(photo Meyer)

Signed and dated, BRUEGEL MDLXV. This work
depicts a month in autumn, as indicated by the colors
and the details, such as the harvested vineyard and the
net for catching birds. Unfortunately, it is in a poor
state of conservation.

24 - WINTER LANDSCAPE WITH BIRD SNARE

Oil on panel, 38 × 56 cm
Brussels, Musées royaux des Beaux-Arts
Delporte Collection

Signed and dated, BRUEGEL M.D.LXV. This pure landscape, which served as an archetype for many seventeenth-century Flemish landscapes, dates from the same year as the Months. There are several variations and copies of this work, whose authenticity is doubted by some scholars.

25 - THE MASSACRE OF THE INNOCENTS

Oil on panel, 111 × 160 cm
Vienna, Kunsthistorisches Museum
(photo Meyer)

This work bears the fragmentary signature BRUEG——
and is dated around 1565 to 1566. Grossmann rejects
it as an autograph, maintaining that the version in
Hampton Court is the original, even though it has been
contaminated by repaintings. A *Massacre of the
Innocents* is cited by Van Mander as being in the
collection of Rudolph II. There are two copies by
Bruegel the Younger dated 1564.

26 - THE CENSUS AT BETHLEHEM

Oil on panel, 116 × 164.5 cm
Brussels, Musées royaux des Beaux-Arts

Signed and dated, BRUEGEL 1566. This scene from the Gospels (Luke II:1-5) is inserted in a depiction of the everyday life of a Flemish village. Acquired by the museum in 1902, this marvelous, lively representation of collective life, with small colored figures against the white snow, gives no particular attention to the blessed couple.

27 - THE ADORATION OF THE MAGI IN THE SNOW

Oil on panel, 35 × 55 cm
Winterthur, Oskar Reinhart Collection

A somewhat illegible inscription on this panel reads
M.D.LXVII BRUEGEL. This work was in the collection
of the French banker Eberhard Jabach who died in
1696, and is precisely described in the inventory of his
possessions. The holy event on the far left does not
interrupt the life of the village in the heavy snowstorm.

28 - WEDDING DANCE IN THE OPEN AIR

Oil on panel, 119 × 157 cm
Detroit, Institute of Arts, City appropriation (30.374)

Dated MDLXVI, this picture was acquired on the English antique market in 1930 in bad condition; it was restored in 1942, dispelling almost every doubt as to its authenticity. However, De Tolnay believes that the original is a miniature in the Uffizi. Numerous copies and replicas of this splendid composition, which initiates Bruegel's scenes of peasant life, are known.

29 - THE CONVERSION OF ST. PAUL

Oil on panel, 108 × 156 cm
Vienna, Kunsthistorisches Museum
(photo Meyer)

Signed and dated, BRUEGEL M.D.LXVII. Here Bruegel has inserted an episode from the Acts of the Apostles (IX, 3) in a magnificent mountain landscape, which some scholars see as an allusion to the Duke of Alba crossing the Alps with his army. The scene of the conversion is reduced to a minimal detail in the central portion of the composition (as in *The Suicide of Saul,* which has an identical format). This work was acquired by the Archduke Ernest in 1594, and later passed to the collection of Rudolph II.

30 - PEASANT WEDDING FEAST

Oil on panel, 114 × 163 cm
Vienna, Kunsthistorisches Museum
(photo Meyer)

The date and signature on this work were lost when a
strip of five cm was cut from the bottom. It probably
dates from 1567, as does the following *Peasant
Wedding Dance,* to which it probably was a
companion piece. This is one of Bruegel's best-known
compositions. The perspective format has suggested to
some critics a derivation from Tintoretto's *Last Supper.*
The Archduke Ernest bought this picture for 150 florins.

31 - PEASANT WEDDING FEAST (detail)

Vienna, Kunsthistorisches Museum

32 - PEASANT WEDDING DANCE

Oil on panel, 114 × 164 cm
Vienna, Kunsthistorisches Museum
(photo Meyer)

Signed BRUEGEL, undated. This work is typical of
Bruegel's late period, when he began to emphasize the
main characters of a scene: the dancing couple, the
monumental bagpipe player. Like many other works in
Vienna, this picture was taken to Paris as part of
Napoleon's booty in 1808, and was returned in 1815.

33 - THE LAND OF COCKAIGNE

Oil on panel, 52 × 78 cm
Munich, Alte Pinakothek
(photo Blauel)

Signed and dated, M.D.LXVII BRUEGEL. This painting depicts *Luilekkerland,* the land of idlers and gluttons of Flemish folk tradition. It was stolen from the imperial collection in Prague by the Swedes in 1648. Its whereabouts were unknown until it reappeared badly repainted in a small antique shop in Vevey, where it was bought for five francs. Restored and reassessed, the Munich museum bought it in 1917 for two hundred thousand Marks.

34 - THE BLIND LEADING THE BLIND

Tempera on canvas, 86 × 154 cm
Naples, Gallerie Nazionali di Capodimonte
(photo Pedicini)

Signed and dated, BRUEGEL M.D.LX.VIII. Like *The Misanthrope,* this work was in the collection of Count G.B. Masi of Parma; in 1611 it was confiscated by the Farnese family, and in 1734 it was transferred to Naples with the Farnese legacy. The allusion here is to the evangelical parable of the blind man led by a blind man who falls in a ditch (Matthew XV:14 and Luke VI:39).

35 - THE BLIND LEADING THE BLIND (detail)

Naples, Gallerie Nazionali di Capodimonte

36 - THE MISANTHROPE

Tempera on canvas, 86 × 85 cm
Naples, Gallerie Nazionali di Capodimonte
(photo Pedicini)

Signed and dated BRUEGEL 1568, an inscription considered by some scholars to be apocryphal. The distich below the two figures reads: ''Since the world is so evil, I dress in mourning.'' The man in the crystal globe (who also appears in *Flemish Proverbs*) symbolizes the world.

Om dat de werelt is soe ongetru
Daer om gha ic inden ru

37 - THE CRIPPLES

Oil on panel, 18 × 21 cm
Paris, The Louvre
(clichés Musées Nationaux Paris)

Signed and dated, BRUEGEL M.D.LXVIII. This panel was donated to the Louvre in 1892 by the art critic Paul Mantz. This disturbing group of five unfortunates remains a mystery, especially with regard to the interpretation of the foxes' tails on the cripples' capes: perhaps they were an emblem of beggars, which later acquired a political meaning.

38 - THE ROBBER OF BIRDS' NESTS

Oil on panel, 59 × 68 cm
Vienna, Kunsthistorisches Museum
(photo Meyer)

Signed and dated, BRUEGEL M.D.LXVIII. This work
was in the collection of Archduke Leopold William,
1659. Like many others of Bruegel's pictures, this
painting illustrates a folk proverb: "He who knows
where the nest is, knows it; he who takes it, owns it."

39 - THE MAGPIE ON THE GALLOWS

Oil on panel, 45.9 × 50.8 cm
Darmstadt, Hessisches Landesmuseum

Signed and dated, BRUEGEL 1568. Van Mander writes that the dying painter left this picture to his wife, and that with the loquacious bird he meant to symbolize that evil tongues deserve the gallows. But there is probably another, much more serious meaning behind this painting, in which Bruegel's pictorial language reaches a marvelous lyrical intensity.

40 - STORM AT SEA

Oil on panel, 70.5 × 97 cm
Vienna, Kunsthistorisches Museum
(photo Meyer)

Unsigned and undated. This painting, which is
probably unfinished, is considered Bruegel's last work,
and therefore dates from 1569. In this case too, the
painter is alluding to a proverb: "The whale who
follows the barrel lets the boat escape." This is perhaps
the panel mentioned in the Stevens Collection in
Antwerp, 1668.

Bruegel's Technique

One must first and foremost stress the impeccable execution of Bruegel's paintings, which reveals a complete mastery of his craft, along with a compositional confidence that is borne out by the almost total lack of *pentimenti* revealed by X rays. All of this was the result of Bruegel's extensive and continual graphic activity, from the drawings from his trip to Italy to the ones with which he incessantly provided the printmaker Cock.

Almost all of Bruegel's paintings are oil on wood panel, with rare additions of tempera, as in *The Land of Cockaigne*. The panels were prepared with a priming of gesso and glue, and a layer of color, which explains the generally satisfactory (in some cases, excellent) state of preservation of his pictures.

His first works, in tempera on canvas with diluted colors, or the gouaches done when Bruegel was working with Clovio have been destroyed by time (the only surviving work of this kind, an *Adoration of the Magi* in Brussels, is extremely deteriorated and colorless), because of the fragility of the canvases and their sensitivity to moisture. The two fortunate exceptions are the temperas in the Capodimonte Museum in Naples.

Bruegel's technique can almost be "read" with the naked eye in the cases when the faded paint (*The Return of the Herd,* the Detroit *Wedding Dance*) allows the preparation, and at times even the drawing, to show through. Bruegel applied his colors in successive thin layers, with very small, almost dry, brushes. This must have been not only a precise process but a very slow one; yet, in the case of the *Months*, Bruegel produced six (or twelve) paintings in the course of a single year, and such speed (writes Grossmann) "is possible only in an artist who is completely master of his technique." In the course of his brief career Bruegel's handling of colors became increasingly masterful; in his last works (*The Robber of Birds' Nests, The Cripples, The Magpie on the Gallows*) he created luminous effects with minute, almost "Impressionistic" brush strokes, anticipating Vermeer's miraculous handling of light.

SELECTED BIBLIOGRAPHY
(in chronological order)

R. VAN BASTELAER and G. H. DE LOO
Pieter Bruegyel l'Ancien son oeuvre et son temps
Brussels, 1907.
M. DVOŘAK
Pieter Bruegel der Ältere
Vienna, 1921.
J. DENUCÉ
Les Galeries d'art à Anvers aux XVIe et XVIIe siècles
Antwerp, 1932.
C. DE TOLNAY
Pierre Bruegel l'Ancien
Brussels, 1935.
G. GLÜCK
Das Bruegel Buch
Vienna, 1936.
M. J. FRIEDLÄNDER
Pieter Bruegel
Brussels, 1937.
G. JEDLIKA
Pieter Bruegel, Der Maler in seiner Zeit
Zurich, 1947.
V. DENIS
Tutta la pittura di Pieter Bruegel
Milan, 1952.
C. DE TOLNAY
The Drawings of Pieter Bruegel the Elder
London-New York, 1952.
G. FAGGIN
Brueghel
Milan, 1953.
R. SALVINI
La pittura fiamminga
Milan, 1958.
F. GROSSMANN
Entry ''Bruegel, Pieter the Elder''
in *Encyclopedia Universale dell'Arte,* Vol. II
Venice-Rome, 1958.
R. L. DELEVOY
Bruegel
Geneva, 1959.
F. GROSSMANN
Bruegel: The Painting. Complete edition
London, 1966.

G. ARPINO and P. BIANCONI
L'opera completa di Bruegel
Milan, 1967.
R. H. MARIJNISSEN and M. SEIDEL
Bruegel
Brussels, 1969.
P. PHILIPPOT
Pittura fiamminga e rinascimento italiano
Turin, 1970.
C. BROWN
Bruegel
London, 1975.
F. DE POLI and E. BACCHESCHI
Bruegel
Milan, 1976.
L. LEBEER
Le incisioni di Pieter Bruegel il Vecchio
Florence, 1976.